UNDONE

One Woman's Journey to Reverse the Curse

UNDONE

One Woman's Journey to Reverse the Curse

Dorothy L. Barcol

ISBN 979-8-9862151-1-2
Printed in the United States of America
Published by FUSION Publishing Group
Butler, Pennsylvania
www.AmyTravisUnlimited.com

Dedication

To my children Ches, Brittany, Shy, and Dylan.

Mom loves you more than you'll ever know.

UNDONE

One Woman's Journey to Reverse the Curse

Foreword

By Jane Efinger-Hayden

At the risk of sounding cliché, the story you are about to read is true.

You will meet a woman who endured atrocities, yet prevailed as resilient, industrious, and entrepreneurial.

I first met Dottie approximately 20 years ago when we were matched with two of her children through the Big Brother/Big Sister Program at Myers Elementary School, the oldest continuously operating school in the United States in Cannelton, Indiana, while I was employed there. She was graciously willing to share her kids (with subsequent grandchildren!) resulting in a wonderful bonus family for us all.

I consider myself fortunate to have had abundant blessings bestowed upon me—a large loving family, a great education, good health, financial stability, many travels, fulfilling/constant employment, and a remarkable 33-year marriage (so far). I'm a proud Air Force brat and an Army dependent.

Two years ago, without hesitation and at the darkest hour in my life, Dottie agreed to provide hospice care for my mom. Her incredible work ethic supplied much-needed care and comfort to my family during my mother's passing.

Even though Dottie struggled at times to obtain or acquire just some of the blessings I found, she is the most optimistic and happy individual you'll ever meet. I'll never forget last Christmas when I had a poinsettia delivered to her home. She told me she'd never had flowers sent to her before. She is always so humble, grateful, and appreciative.

Her sharing spirit, kindness, and immense love have no bounds where her family and friends are concerned. She is the most unassuming, down-to-earth, and entertaining person to be around.

So, settle in and take a ride with her that will surely garner empathy (from some), sympathy, and amazement (from all) as you cheer Dottie on during her incredible journey.

This is my friend, Dottie—a survivor.

With so much admiration,

Mrs. Jane Efinger-Hayden

1.

I

Curse of the Penny Loafer Shoe

Love applies to so many parts of life. We all want love and to be loved. Maybe it was love, maybe it was not love, that brought me into this world the day before Valentine's Day, 1966. My Mom, Glenda, gave me the name Dorothy after my dad's mother even though she divorced him when I was two. I was the third of my mom's children. First Angie, then Bobby, then me, and six years later, Amy.

Smells are strong memories. I read once about a study that smells create the strongest memories. I remember the smells of childhood. My earliest memories were the sporadic few days of daycare or some place that Mom would take me to when she would come and get me. I had a large stuffed snoopy that was bigger than life. I would lie next to my snoopy in a baby bed at daycare or a babysitter's. I can still remember the smell of Snoopy. Mom wasn't consistent but Snoopy was always there. Mom was in barber school, and I stayed a lot at a sitter's house. I remember the park close by and the smell of coffee. It always smelled like coffee. I think I was maybe seven during those coffee-smelling memories.

I would go to the park and play because it was right by the babysitter's house. I would hear sounds of ambulances and police cars going around town and when I heard the sound, I would get scared. I would fall to the ground and cry. I cried because I thought they were coming for my Mom. I would think that she was hurt or that something had happened to her. Looking back, I now know why I cried and fell to the ground so many times hearing the sounds.

When my mother first divorced my father, I lived with my Great-Grandma, Floria. Floria smelled like Vic Vapo-rub. She had arthritic fingers and I remember falling asleep in her bed with her feather filled mattress and the quilts she made. Since she came from Germany, I called her "Old Grandma" or "Old Maw." I didn't think of it as an insult. When I got older, I found out that "Old Maw" or "Oma" was German for Grandma. My Oma was the angel who saved me in so many ways. I felt her love and protection as complete as the Vic's she would rub me down with from head to toe.

I was probably three when I moved in with Old Maw. We would listen to Oral Roberts preaching through the old-fashioned radio with the hearing aids that would whistle. She would hold my hands while praying with the sermons. My Oma shared her memories with me from her childhood: Cinnamon and brown and white sugars were sprinkled on the bowls of oatmeal that my Old Maw made me. I found out later that this was one of her favorite things to eat as a child. If it wasn't oatmeal for breakfast, it was an egg on Friday with mustard and two pieces of toast.

Even though I loved Old Maw, I loved my mom and missed her all the time. I was so excited when she would come to visit Old Maw's, bringing me a bag of toys. I don't remember the toys, just the excitement of seeing my mom.

Old Maw had a remedy for everything. If my stomach hurt, it was butter from the fridge. If I had a cold or a sore throat, she would bake onions in the oven and have me inhale their smell like the Vic's Vapo-rub before I ate them. When I would do something bad my Old Maw would tell me in her stern voice to go out back of the old shotgun house in Covington Kentucky. I would have to get a switch, not a little switch or I knew what would happen, and she would bust my butt so hard. It wasn't the pain of the whipping that hurt. It was that I had done something wrong that she didn't like. So many of the safe adults in my life would leave and I didn't want to do anything that would cause me to lose my Old Maw.

I thought my Old Maw's house was my safe place. One night when I was falling asleep next to my Old Maw surrounded by her and the smell of Vic's Vapo-rub I hear a thud or the sound of something falling. I didn't know what it was. I climbed over my Old Maw, she was a really large lady. I went into the hall to find a brown shoe. It was a penny loafer but at four, I didn't know that and it wasn't until years later when I would tell my story that I found out what that brown shoe was called.

My cousin, my second cousin, I think, was standing there. I was too young to even know how we were related. My cousin would come and go as he pleased and do what he wanted to at Old Ma's house. "Bring it here, Dottie". His stern voice was coming from the living room. This night would start a pattern that felt like it was repeated a million times, on a million other nights.

When I would bring him the shoe as his stern voice demanded, he would be lying on that old scratchy green sofa that I hated. He would prop me up next to him as he pulled down his pajama pants, slipping his hands to his private parts, his other hand in my panties. I remember him with his hand going up and down in his pajama pants as he would put his other hand all over a place where his hand should never have been. He would always have something come out of his pajamas that was looking really gross to me. As I know now it was him masturbating and molesting me. I hated that sofa and I hated those nights when he would come to stay at Old Maw's house.

The curse of the brown penny loafer shoe happened to my sister Angie, too. Now, as a woman in my 50s, I think back on that time. I carry the memories of these penny loafer nights with me. I remember them like I remember so many things about my childhood. It's part of my childhood.

I missed my Mom so much. I wanted my Mom to come back and see me. My cousin knew this and used it against me. He would remind me to do what he said or he would make sure my Mom never, ever came back to see me. That's all I wanted was my Mom. Sometimes days, weeks, months years would go by and I let him do what he wanted to so one day I might be able to see my Mom again.

I had another cousin live upstairs from my Old Maw whose name was Sue. She was dark and beautiful, either Indian or half Indian. One day, in second grade which would have been 8 years old, while walking to school Sue stopped and said "I have an idea. Do you want to go?" I agreed and we walked all over the streets of Covington.

I was so tired and it was so hot. We went to a lot of stores that I can't even name but one, Woolworths, I remember. Woolworths stood out because of the cool place to eat and a little booth to take your picture. I would like to have taken my picture, but I never had much money except when my Old Maw would give me a nickel to go pick up her medicine about six blocks away at the pharmacy/candy store. That nickel always bought me a lot of candy in my little brown paper bag.

My cousin would tell me to keep secrets. I was supposed to have gone to school and Sue had taken me to play hooky. Sue was looking in Woolworth's jewelry section looking at all the beautiful, shiny jewelry. I guess it was getting close to the time that school would be over because she suddenly said, "Come on let's go you're going to be late". I remember the red balloon she bought me and how when I would walk, it would float up and down with the swinging of my arm that it was tied to.

We were getting close to the house so she said "Hey, we've got to get rid of the balloon. We can't let anybody know where we have a been."

On the way home that day after skipping school and after letting my balloon go, I went to my babysitter's house. (Sometimes my Mom would pick me up for a visit from my old grandma's house. We would stay with friends of hers or at babysitters. I never really knew where we would be.) It really wasn't a house. It was a little store off of Main Street in Covington, right around the corner. It's called

Main Strauss now and is all fixed up with a lot of shops and little bars and restaurants.

It's hard to remember all the details of that day. As I walked into the little store which is about the size of a small bedroom seemed like my babysitter who owned the store asked me how my day was, I said it was good. Apparently, some of my friends told her what I have done that day. I wasn't a good liar, and I could tell by the expression on her face that I might be in trouble.

For some reason, this babysitter felt the need to humiliate me. She wasn't my mother, and she wasn't even a relative. But when she when discovered that I had lied about what I had done that day, she made a spectacle of me. There was a cigarette vending machine in the store where you could pull a knob and get the cigarettes that you wanted. She put me on top of that cigarette machine, put a diaper on me, and the baby bottle next to me. She had me hold a poster that had "me baby, me play hooky from school" written on it. This was devastating for an eight-year-old.

It was a popular little store with good cheap candy so all my friends from school would come to this little store. They would be coming to get what they thought their moms and dads would want them to get and, if they were lucky, they would have an extra $.50 to spend on candy.

It seemed like I was on top of that cigarette machine for hours. At some point, my older sister, Angie, came and before she could get into the store, my babysitter quickly locked the front door. I didn't know why until I heard my sister screaming at the top of her lungs. She was yelling "Get my sister down from there right now!" She was very mad. I was her baby sister and she was protecting me. She beat and beat on the door, and it seemed like they would never let her in.

The kids were still laughing and making fun of me the next day when I was back at school. Kids can be cruel. I laughed along with them. That's what you do, isn't it? Rather than let them see that it hurts. Or to cry. Or to stop it. You say nothing.

When I would finally go on outings with my mom or when I got to spend a few days, it was never happy and peaceful. I really wanted it to be because of the abuse I took when I wasn't with her, but it never was. I can remember a few times when my mom came to pick me up and we would go stay at her new apartment. There would be different men in and out and lots of people drinking and doing drugs. I would see Mom sometimes in bed with a man having sex. I was young but I knew what was going on because of the things that happened when I was younger. I thought it was a sign of love.

Every time I was hoping she would have a room for me and my brother Bobby, who always stayed with my dad and who I never really saw much of, but she didn't. My sister Angie wouldn't go with us because she stayed with my Grandma Margaret who was Old Maw's daughter.

After people were drinking and doing drugs it seems like there was always fighting and somebody getting hurt, and blood all over the place. I've seen my mom get hit by many men in her lifetime. I was always scared when I heard the sirens, and then the ambulances would come. Those sirens would take Mom sometimes. Sometimes those sirens would take the other people. It was either an ambulance or the police, or both.

like and how wonderful it would be with all the irons and ironing boards in Heaven. Wow.

There was a friend of mine in school who had long red hair. She hardly ever brushed it and she had freckles. More freckles than me and I had a lot of freckles when I was little. Everybody would tell me that they were beauty marks. Yeah, right. She was a chubby little girl and she lived about six or seven blocks away from my mom's. One afternoon my mom went to work or somewhere, we never really knew for how long or when she would come back. Or, even, who she would come back with. I don't remember who was watching us that day but what I do remember is my little chunky, redheaded friend from school didn't get anything from Santa that year. I had always thought there was a Santa and when I found out that my friend didn't get anything for Christmas, I loaded up my wagon my beautiful red wagon with my fridge, ironing board, and, yes, my iron.

The sidewalks in Covington were always uneven. The cobblestone streets made a bumpy ride with my wagon piled with my Christmas valuables. I had to reposition my load, but I made it there. I knocked on her door and told my friend "Hey, Santa left these at my house for you. He said he got the wrong address so here you go." I walked home feeling so good about myself. So happy that I did something good for somebody.

My mom was not happy. She said, "do you know how hard I had to work for that do you know how many men I had to dance for to get that shit!!" I got whipped and whipped and whipped it seem like it would never end. You would think I had learned my lesson from that ass whipping. Nope. I didn't. It just got worse as I grew up.

2

Tale of Two Moms

Glenda Lee Young was born on October 10th, 1943, during World War II. Her mom, Grandma Margaret, was a large woman. She wasn't the nicest; actually, she was a very selfish woman, but she was also generous in her own way. Grandma Margaret worked as a nurse at the tuberculosis center in northern Kentucky. I suppose we all are dependent on things that happen to us and things that our parents do to shape our childhood. My Mom's life was shaped by my grandma's life. Mom would say that Grandma was hard on her and whipped her a lot. She didn't show much love or affection to her daughter, my mom. Mom was beautiful in the pictures I saw of her when she was a young girl. She looked like Priscilla Presley with her dark, almost black hair.

Grandma Margaret belonged to a Pentecostal church. When I visited her, she always took me there every day that the doors were open. She would go to every funeral in town, even if she didn't know the person that passed away. Usually, during those funerals, families would have dinner and people would bring casseroles and different contributions that they had made. Grandma Margret was a diabetic but that didn't stop her from overeating just to overeat.

Even though Grandma Margaret married several times (it could have been four husbands, I can't be sure), my mom was an only child. She was repeatedly abused by one of Grandma Margaret's husbands who had raped my mom many times. One of those times when mom was raped, she became pregnant with my older sister Angie. Mom tried to tell Grandma Margret what had happened, but Grandma Margret didn't believe her. Or maybe she did believe her and didn't want to do anything about it. I never knew whether my grandma didn't know what to do about it and thought it was easier to think that my mom was lying or for some other reason. I can't figure it out. I'm sure times were different then. The fear of embarrassment outweighed Grandma Margret's decision to do the right thing for my mother.

After Mom gave birth to Angie on March 28, 1961, she moved in with my Dad. Grandma Margret took Angie and raised her with Henry, her last husband. Henry was an old, retired coal miner. Grandpa Henry wore overalls every day and drank a lot. When he would get drunk, he would yell and holler at Grandma Margret after she had come home from church. He was a mean drunk, but it didn't appear to bother Grandma Margret. She would just pray for the devil to leave his soul and then go about her way. She was used to it. Or, maybe she felt she deserved it for being so mean all the time. I know that's awful to say—since nobody deserves to be treated terribly. Maybe Grandma Margaret acted mean because so many people treated her that way. Either way, Grandma Margaret had a hard life.

Angie

My Mom couldn't have been ready to have Angie and Grandma Margaret may have been angry about having to raise a baby girl in her older years. Maybe this was Grandma Margaret being nice in her own way because she left Angie's father who had raped my mom. After all, she did take on raising Angie. Life is filled with "maybes" and how hard it is to understand why people do the things they do—and how it shapes our lives.

When I lived with Ole Grandma, Angie lived with Grandma Margaret. Angie was four years older than me. She was so pretty with long blonde hair and blue eyes. She lived behind the grade school we attended; an alley separated her house and the school building. Angie and I rode our bikes up and down the alley into Goebbel's park across the street. I held the prestigious Jack's Champion title for a couple of years! I was the Hula hoop champion, too. We enjoyed the free lunch bags that they gave out to the kids at the park. I always looked forward to the brown paper bag lunches after swimming all day. We would be hungry and thirsty, and those lunch bags were just the right thing we needed.

I remember visiting Angie when she was about twelve years old, and I was eight. When I slept in Angie's bedroom, she would make me sleep on the side against the wall. That was fine with me because that's where I slept when I was at Old Grandma's house. The only problem was that Angie had a bed-wetting problem. When she peed on the bed, she would roll me over to her spot where she had peed. I'd wake up when I felt wetness under me and would grab the rug next to the bed on the floor and put it under me till morning. For the longest time, I thought it was me who had the problem peeing the bed. When I finally realized it wasn't me, I got mad at Angie and told her to stop making it look like it was me. She still did this for many more years. Looking back at that now, I wondered why a girl her age would still have been wetting the bed. Maybe things were going on in her life that she never told me about.

Angie's life didn't get any easier as she got older, partly because of her own choices. Angie had a reputation for being very stubborn. She was so spoiled by Grandma Margret and didn't want to listen to anyone. Grandma Margaret always gave her everything she wanted and took care of all her needs. So, when Angie was 13, she convinced Grandma Margaret to allow her to hang out with Mom. They would go to parties together! This single decision led to many bad choices which would haunt Angie for years to come. As a result of being exposed to this lifestyle, Angie got involved in drugs and drinking.

Angie met a man named Jesse at one of these parties who rode a motorcycle. He was in a motorcycle gang in Covington, Kentucky, but I don't remember the name of the gang. I do remember that he was much older than Angie when they got together. Not surprisingly, Angie got pregnant soon after they started dating. Angie was fourteen years old. After the baby was born, Angie married Jesse. She told me after the wedding ceremony was over, Jesse's buddies would line up one by one in a row on each side of the happy newlyweds. This was part of his initiation. The couple walked together hand in hand while Jesse's buddies dropped drugs and drinks into their mouths. She told me they had to take everything they gave them while walking through the line. I'm sure they slept well that night.

Jesse was a nice good-looking fella, and they made a good-looking couple. Angie gave birth to a beautiful baby girl named Brandy. She named Brandy after the song "Brandy (you're a fine girl)" released by Looking Glass in 1972. Brandy bore my mom's middle name, Lee. Brandy had dark hair like her dad. She was a good baby and Angie and Jesse loved her dearly. But, Angie—being so young—needed to sow her oats. She left her husband and baby to party and do whatever she wanted. Jessie didn't mind too much; he and Brandy would chill at his Mom's house waiting until she came home a few days later.

Stripped

Mom struggled with many mental issues. I guess that's to be expected with all the drugs and the abuse from her mom and stepdad. Mom turned to drugs to escape all of it. She wasn't much of a drinker, but she enjoyed her drugs and the men she got to meet while being a stripper around town. Mom was beautiful and very popular; she had some good dance moves. (Mom would twerk at the family get-togethers. She was 73 when she passed and I'm sure she is twerking up in heaven.)

A lot of men enjoyed the company of my mom. She had the gift of gab. She had good conversations with the men in the clubs. She was a good listener, too, whenever you needed someone to talk to.

Mom was one of the best strippers around. One time they sent her to North Carolina to work at a special bar or something. I remember flying in an airplane with her. She let me sit by the window since it was the first time I had ever been on a plane. When we arrived at the place where she worked, I got to sit at the bar before the bar opened. I felt like the luckiest kid in the world. I got all the pretzels and chips I could eat. They even gave me a little straw to put in my soda pop. It was the same kind they put in mixed drinks they made for the real customers. All the girls who worked there would always come and talk to me and tell me how cute and sweet I was. They would tell me I was very shy. When the music would start and the people came into the club, I would go to the back of the bar where the girls got dressed and got all their make-up on. Mom would always have me stay there when she went out to dance. I thought it was fun. I got to meet a lot of people. I would fall asleep on a bench somewhere until it was time to go.

I don't ever remember living with Mom, only visiting her. My safe place was with my Old Grandma but in my heart, I always wanted to be with my mom. Maybe that's every child's yearning. They always want their mom. Maybe I felt sorry for her, too. I needed to be there to help take care of her.

As a result of her mental issues, Mom had another personality which she referred to as Shane. I wonder if that's because of all the trauma that happened when she was so young. I think between being raped by her stepdad and everything else which happened to her as a child, she developed a split personality as a coping mechanism. When my mom would become Shane, she became a completely different person. She would say things like "moon is your dad and is an Indian. You are an Indian. Your dad spent time in prison. When he got out, I met him, and we had sex in a field under a full moon. So that's why I named you Moon." I always just laughed it off.

I enjoyed visiting mom at this house where she lived off and on. Someone had painted the Flintstones cartoon characters on the cabinets in the kitchen, so I would look at the Flintstones and draw them exactly how they were with the papers and crayons mom would give me. Mom loved my artwork. She was always impressed, and so proud of my talents at such a young age.

Many times, however, when Mom picked me up, *or should I say when Shane would pick me up*, I was scared and nervous. I didn't know what was going to happen that day. Her face looked completely different. She wasn't the beautiful mom that I knew and wanted to be with. I had no idea when Shane would be violent or just plain nuts.

Apparently, Shane had many adventures. Grandma Margret would look all over town to find Shane at the bars or motels. When mom spent a lot of time doing drugs, she would turn into Shane. When Grandma Margret found Shane, she would have to take her to the hospital. Sometimes the police would come to my house. I remember Shane being handcuffed and taken to the hospital. She would wait forever for an evaluation so she could be placed in the mental institution.

For years it was the same pattern over and over. We would go look for Shane up and down the streets of Covington and she would always be at a bar with some sort of hat on or something covering her hair. Shane would always be organizing her things over and over. She would be telling others about the "jobs" she had in the past. For example, she talked about the time she worked for the FBI as a special agent and how she would fly all over the place, working for the President of the United States. She recited her Social Security number for her special FBI ID number over and over and would tell everybody else she was an expert in taekwondo. She said she would use it on anybody who would try to hurt her or the President.

The more drugs mom would do, the more times we would meet Shane. I didn't like Shane. I always knew what would come after finding her. Seeing my mom handcuffed by the police and watching that expression on her face terrified me. After years of Grandma Margret picking Shane up and taking her to the hospital or calling the police, the torch was passed to my sister Angie. Angie became of age and it was her turn to take over. Angie and Mom had such a good relationship of love and drugs that Angie hated taking Shane to the hospital. Her drug buddy would be gone, and Angie would feel sad.

When Shane appeared, I knew Mom had been getting high again. Mom shot up meth, speed, pills, whatever she could afford or find. She shot up dope in every part of her body wherever she could. She would sometimes talk to other people about where she shot up. She couldn't hit the right vein so she would have to do it in her neck or her leg. Hearing that depressed me when I had to listen to them all talk about getting high. I wish I could have listened to a voice of a mom talking to friends about the things in life like her children, their accomplishments, and what things they did.

Instead, mom taught me a lot of things unintentionally by having to watch her. Even at a young age, I knew I never wanted to do drugs because of the things I witnessed. I can't even count how many times I had to search for her, trick her into getting in my car, and put her in a mental hospital until her medication would all be back where it needed to be. Sometimes it would take a few months for mom to be released.

When we visited mom at the hospital it would always be like a field trip. Shane was all drama. She would get mad and want to hurt someone if they didn't do what she wanted. Shane came from a place deep in the back of Mom's mind from all the pain from the abuse that she went through in her life. I knew she had a bad life. She didn't get much love or compassion from her family. The lack of affection can make a person become someone they don't want to be. Or, in Mom's case, a person they don't even know.

When I was at Old Grandma's, I never knew who would be picking me up or when I would get picked up. I got used to living with Old Grandma. I enjoyed it. I knew I was OK there. When my mom would pick me up, or Shane, I never knew what to expect. It always led to a crazy experience. I remember on several occasions going to this big Goodwill store (or another thrift store) parking lot. There was a big dumpster-like metal box where people would take their clothes and things they no longer wanted. Sometime later it would be cleaned out and taken to a thrift store, sorted through, and priced to sell.

Mom would say, "Hey, let's find us a treasure." I was around five and still pretty tiny, so she lifted me up to the swinging door so I could crawl into the dumpster. It was fun—at first—looking for shoes that matched, a jacket to wear, or maybe a toy. Sometimes it would be full, and I didn't have to jump down in it, but sometimes it was empty. I hated when that happened. I would have to stack a bunch of things on top of each other so I could reach the swinging door and mom could help me out of the dumpster.

The donation dumpster was always very dark. I could hardly see unless mom held the swinging door open. I'd find a shoe that was mom's size she would tell me to keep looking for the other shoe. So, I kept looking and moving things around and digging for that treasure because I wanted her to be proud of me for finding that other shoe.

My memories of Mom and Shane are scattered up and down. I don't always remember how old I was. I just remember I had to be under the age of ten because at age ten my dad got custody of me. One time while visiting mom at the little apartment she rented, she had me hold one side of a rubber band so she could tie it around her arm. Mom used needles to get drugs into her system faster. That way she could have that buzz she craved. My sister Angie would say "Mom, don't make her do that. I will do it for you." I didn't know anything was wrong. I was just doing what Mom wanted me to do. That always made me feel good to make her happy.

My Dad and Stepmom never allowed me to go with my mom after I moved in with them. I sort of understood why, but it also broke my heart. I always felt sorry for my mom. I knew down deep she loved us.

I do have some good memories of my mom, though. When I was twelve years old, my mom, Shane, knocked on the door of my dad's house. In her hands were two presents: one was for my brother, Bobby. It was a little army figure, a GI Joe. The other gift was a tube of paint for me; just one little, small tube of paint, the kind of paint that you would use to paint-by-numbers or to paint a model car.

I didn't get to talk to my mom that day. I peeked out of my bedroom door and heard them talking. That tube of paint meant more than any gift that I could've ever had in life because it was given to me by someone that my mom didn't know (well, not really). It was from Shane, but Shane knew my mom loved us. She (Shane) knew I loved to draw and paint. I knew at that moment that Bobby and I were etched deep in my mom's brain and heart. This remains one of the best memories I have of my mom from my childhood.

Parenting the Parent

When I turned eighteen, technically an adult, my sister Angie told me that it was now my turn to carry the torch. I didn't understand what my sister Angie meant by that at the time, but it turned out to be a big responsibility. A responsibility that I did not like. It's a sad thing that I had to do when Mom became Shane. Even when mom was Glenda she really wasn't like a real mom. She never taught me how to do things like cooking, cleaning, or how it is to be treated by a man. She didn't teach me how to act properly or any of the things that mothers teach their daughters.

Shane was often violent. She would go to the bars and tell her stories to her friends that would sit and listen until they couldn't take her antics anymore. I would get a call in the middle of the night to come to pick her up. They would tell me, "Dottie, your mom's here, and can you pick her up, she's done it again."

The worst call I got was around 7:30 in the morning one January. The year was 2012 and I was 45 years old and living in Cannelton, IN. I remember it being so cold out. I heard the familiar, dreaded knock on the door. I never locked my door so usually, everybody just walked into my house so I knew it might be something important. It was the police.

When I saw the police at my door, I even thought for a second, *did I do something wrong?* The officer said "Dottie, your mom is at the hospital you need to go there now. We found her over in the parking lot at the Cotton Mill Apartments crawling on the ground. We couldn't get up. Her body temperature is very low, and her condition is not good. You need to go right now."

I wasn't very worried at that moment. I was just mad that I knew she was doing drugs again and got herself in that position. I always thought that her drug use was so selfish. It was selfish of her to get high because other things in life, like her children, didn't make her high. I knew her children didn't make her happy like the needle that went into her arm with the meth and all the other dope. She used drugs so much that she didn't have any good veins left. It seemed selfish that rather than her taking care of me, I had to take care of her.

Mom recovered after this episode, as she always did. But this time I knew I needed to crack down on her. As the disciplined one, I would need to parent her. I began monitoring her all the time, watching who she hung with and what she did . . . everything. This overwhelmed me. I was a single mother myself working three to four jobs at a time while raising four kids.

I never knew mom in a way that a child would get to know their mom. I would cry for her as a child. In my mind, I thought a mom should be a protector from all evil that happens to you. That certainly wasn't the case in my family.

I checked on mom many times at her house. I would bring her groceries or whatever she needed. I tried to get her to give me her disability check card, but she never let me have it. I eventually took her card to make sure she paid her bills and no one took advantage of her. She was a very independent woman with tons of friends and many people loved to hang around with her. I don't know if it was the drugs they had in common, or if mom was just a fun person to hang with.

Even though Angie handed off the responsibility of babysitting mom to me, she loved her very much. Mom had married five times but would always live with Angie in between relationships. They grew up more like sisters than mom and daughter. Angie took great care of her, but more than that, they were best friends.

3

Dirty Little Secrets

My dad was a quiet man. He worked as much as he drank, and he did both a lot. I remember that he loved cooking. I never really stayed with my Dad much before he got custody of me when I was about ten or eleven years old. In fact, he didn't pick me up for a visit or come to see me regularly. Sure, I'd see him here and there, but nothing consistent. So, it felt weird when I was told I was going to go live with him.

I didn't want to live with him at first because I didn't want to leave my Old Grandma—even with the abuse that was secretly going on. But after I thought about it, I thought it might be a way to escape the abuse, even though leaving Old Grandma was hard and sad.

My first day with Dad and his wife Fran was exciting because I had never gone school shopping before. We all went to the store to get new clothes for me and did all of that stuff normal people do, but I had never gotten to do. My Stepmom had two beautiful daughters; they were good at sports and good at everything. I was so jealous of them, but I loved them. They loved me too, and we all got along.

During the shopping experience, I was nervous because I didn't know what to do. I just knew what I liked to wear and what I felt comfortable in. What I got was the total opposite. Little did I know that this was the beginning of one of the most horrible parts of my life. I left the store with the ugliest pair of checkered polyester bell-bottom pants and a jacket to match. These were the ugliest pair of pants ever made in the world. As I walked, I tried to feel grateful. I didn't want to hurt anyone's feelings. On the way out of the store, there was a bubblegum machine, I had some change and put it in, hoping to win a good prize. I got the coolest necklace and I wore it with my new outfit on the first day of school. I walked into the school as if I were John Travolta getting ready to bust some cool dance moves from the movie Saturday Night Fever. I was rocking that outfit, even though I felt like a clown.

My dad knew that I didn't like my Stepmom very much, so he always tried to pay a little bit more attention to me. He knew I was sad being away from Old Grandma and all of the new surroundings. It was hard getting used to all the new rules and everything else going on.

When I left Old Grandma's I thought I had left the sexual abuse behind. Dad began drinking more and more and came home late at night. I knew what was going to happen when he would come home drunk. About twice a week Dad would sneak quietly into my bedroom and sit next to me on the bed. Then he would begin to put his hands up my night shirt while he thought I was sleeping. I would act like I was getting all adjusted in my sleep. I would turn around and try to make him think I was going to wake up. No matter which way I turned, he always found his way to molest me. When he put his hands up my shirt, he always grabbed my breast and pinched my nipples. To this day I have flashbacks when I am touched there as he did. I would roll over and try to make him stop, but he didn't. He then put his hand in my panties. I still would try to make him think I was sleeping. I was too embarrassed to face him the next day. When morning came, I always acted like I knew nothing.

Dad started molesting me a few months after I moved in with him and my Stepmom. My stepsister Kay would be in the twin bed next to mine and he would do the same to her. Kay and I didn't discuss what he was doing to us for a few years. I was scared to tell anyone. At first, I thought this is what happens to girls. I thought it was normal. I knew I would get in trouble if I told on him. My stepmom would be very mad. I also thought it would hurt my dad's feelings if I told her what he did to us. It's the logic of a child. I mean, here's my dad raping me and I'm worried about hurting his feelings.

Many times, while watching TV I would lay on the floor in the living room. I would be watching a movie on Lifetime about a child being sexually abused and my dad would be sitting on the couch watching it, too. I had to pretend like nothing ever happened because I remembered that I was pretending to be sleeping. I'm sure he had his suspicions sometimes that I was pretending, or maybe not. I don't think anybody could sleep through that. It was horrible! My Dad, my savior, my hero who saved me from the bad man that hurt me while I was living with my Old Grandma was doing the same thing to me. I had thought I was leaving that behind—those disgusting things which men had done to me. I felt like I just had to accept it.

I hated bedtime because that meant I had to give my dad a kiss good night and hug him. I had a disgusting feeling inside me every time I had to hug him which it's so hard to explain. It's a feeling of filth and ugliness inside me that was the same feeling as when the bad stuff was happening. It made me feel worthless. Did I deserve this? Did I ask for this? Of course not. I was so young, and I didn't want it to happen. I just wanted to see my mom.

As I got older and matured into a teenager, the abuse didn't slow down with my Dad. The only different thing, however, was that I developed feelings in my body that I didn't know much about. I never experienced anything like that. The feelings on the parts of my body when my dad touched them created a good sensation and this was very confusing. This made me even feel worse inside because now I felt guilty. After all, it felt good—and bad—at the same time.

Sometimes, I would go stay with a friend Laura who I went to school with. I went to Holmes high school in Covington, which is a forty-five-minute drive from my dad's apartment.

Laura's Mom was cool as hell. She would always give us money when she got her social security check on the first of the month. Laura and I would go buy a Barq's© root beer and Grippos© chips. Grippos© were the best chips ever made. And they were made in Covington close to where she lived. Laura and I would have so much fun. We would sneak out of her house at night and meet the boys behind the floodwall. We would sit and talk to them and make out with them.

At an early age, I thought that sex was just normal, that all kids must have parents who did that to them too. I became pregnant at sixteen with one of the local boys and I was very scared. I didn't know what to do. I knew my stepmom would kill me if she ever found out. I couldn't have this baby! I would punch myself in the belly, run like crazy, jump up and down, and do anything to try to have a miscarriage. I wanted to get rid of this pregnancy. I was young I didn't know what I was doing. I just knew I couldn't have this child.

My brain kept telling me my stepmom would beat me. I was helping a friend move furniture up to the second-floor apartment and I remember thinking "this will help me to miscarry." I carried the heaviest furniture I could lift. Up the stairs, I went. Seemed like to me I went up and down the steps a hundred times always carrying something heavy. About an hour into the move, I felt something going on in my stomach, something wasn't right so I went to the restroom. I stood there while blood poured out of me. It was like pieces of flesh falling out all over the floor. Pieces of things that weren't recognizable came out of me and blood was everywhere. I got really scared. Yes, I wanted this to happen, but I didn't think it would be like this. I yelled to my friend Laura who I hadn't told that I was pregnant.

The hospital, fortunately, was right across the street from my friend's apartment. Laura helped me walk to the hospital. I had put a towel in between my legs with my pants still on. I got what I wanted, a miscarriage. But my gosh, I thought I was dying. I felt selfish and scared. That was a real baby inside me, and I didn't let it live. I was wrong. I knew I should have gone about it the right way but in my abused mind, there was no right way.

I was bleeding so badly that they had to do a procedure in the emergency room. They put a vacuum-like thing inside me where I was bleeding. It sucked out all the blood and all the baby parts that I destroyed. Laura went home so she wouldn't get in trouble for being out past dark. I was alone in the emergency room going through all of this. She told her Mom I went back home. The hospital gave me a room upstairs because I got sick and ran a high fever for a few days. I was all alone until the day I was released. When I was admitted I told them I was 18 but they discovered my real age. I had to have a parent pick me up. My stepmother picked me up and it was not a good day. Even though I tried to keep it from her, she found out anyway. I hated myself so much after that. Self-hatred is something that eats up a person and causes me to do things that I shouldn't do.

A few months later, I finally got to enjoy Spring Break with my mom, Angie, Amy, Grandma Margret, and best of all, Old Grandma. I went to visit mom for a night. She lived in an upstairs apartment in a little town named Cannelton, Indiana. Mom always had her friends over. Some crazy, some cool, and some, well, there are no words for them. Mostly, her friends were good. They were good-hearted people even though their choices may have been different. They were good company for my mom, even when they did drugs. Being around people doing drugs was what I was used to.

There was this one guy at my mom's that was talking with people and drinking. Everyone was drinking but me. I was tired so I went to take a nap on my mom's living room floor. I felt someone touching me I turned around and that guy had a knife. He told me not to say anything. So I didn't make a sound. I knew what he wanted—just like all the rest. I don't remember the act of the rape. I just remember the beginning of it and after I just blocked it out.

My visit with my mom and my mom's family ended and it was time to go back home to my dad's... or I should say to hell. Fall was in the air, and I loved the Fall. I still do. I was in eleventh grade and taking welding classes at a new vocational school in Covington next to where I went to high school. I only took the welding class because all the cute guys were taking the class too. I was a really good welder.

During my short week visiting, I also met a man named John who was older. He was a pig farmer. He was a silly, funny, cute man. We went out a couple of times. One time we went to the drive-in movie and had sex in his truck. I thought I was in love. Boy, I was so wrong.

I started feeling a little different. I was tired and my body had changed. I went to a free clinic to get a pregnancy test and I was pregnant, again! I was about five months along and I was scared. This time I really didn't care. Maybe it was my way to escape from the hell that I was living. Maybe after having this baby, I would know what real love was and what it felt like to have someone love me.

When I was about six months pregnant, my stepmom called me into her bedroom. She was always lying in her bed giving me chores and things to do to make me feel bad or unhappy. She and dad rarely got out of bed. "Bring me this. Bring me that." I tried to make her coffee perfect because I wanted praise from her, but I didn't get the love, praise, and approval that I needed. Dad's coffee was easy, black. As I was leaving the room after delivering coffee, my Stepmother asked me if I was pregnant. She didn't ask it in a kind, loving way. I could've passed out right there on the bedroom floor. I took a deep breath and turned around, looked her in her eyes, and said "yes, I am. I am pregnant." I expected her to beat me for it, but she seemed kind of happy about it. That freaked me out because she was never happy about anything, especially when it came to me. A little bit of attention is better than no attention. I'll take what I can get.

It was so cold that winter when I was pregnant, and my due date was at the end of January. I had doctors' appointments once a month at first. When I got closer to the due date, I had to go once a week. We had so much snow that winter and I had to walk a long way to the doctors' office clinic. It was probably about four miles from the apartment building where we lived. I would bundle up. I knew I'd be cold but I could not ask my Stepmom or Dad for a ride. They just didn't do that kind of thing. I would ask many times, the answer would always be the same. They would say that they didn't have time, or they were sleepy, or they had to work. Always some excuse, so eventually I didn't even bother to ask. I just walked where I had to go.

While walking to my appointments, I would think about how wonderful this baby is going to be in my life. I didn't know if it was a boy or a girl and it didn't matter to me. At first, I thought about wanting this baby to be a boy. A boy to be the oldest and to be the protector of his future younger siblings. On Super Bowl Sunday, January 1984, Francheska was born. Yes, Francheska. Fran thought I named her after her. I told her that so she would love me more. Actually, I got the name from a beautiful Mexican woman off of General Hospital. (I loved Luke and Laura.)

I took Francheska home, back to my dad and stepmom's apartment, and stayed in my little room where I had for so many years. It was a small two-bedroom apartment and being a first-time mom was hard and I was tired and grumpy. I fixed up my room the best I could. I kept my baby in a little bassinet right next to my bed. I would wake up and make sure she was breathing. I didn't have much stuff for her. I didn't have a baby shower. It always made me sad not to have anyone care enough to have one for me, but I got used to always doing for people and they don't give back in any way at all. I say it's OK but it's really not. Someone should have given me one.

My Stepmom always made me take her work clothes down to the laundry room in the basement of the apartment. I had to make sure I always got her work clothes out of the dryer as soon as they dried so I could put a crease in her pants. I wasn't allowed to wash my clothes, so I had to wash mine in the bathtub. I was OK with that. I thought it was pretty cool having a clothesline in my bedroom. My hands were a little sore and had calluses, too. After the baby was born, I could wash her clothes and she went through them quickly. I'd change her all the time. She was my whole world and still is. I nicknamed her Ches like the game but only one S. My Stepmom loved Francheska, in her own way, I guess.

4

Cinderella's Evil Stepmom

My stepmom Fran was a nurse. She was an LPN and worked the night shift and slept all day. You would think that people who go into nursing would be kind, caring people. But basically, she just gave patients medicine as she was instructed.

My Dad and Fran had a little boy named Robby. He was a skinny little boy with white-blonde hair. He was spoiled and got everything he wanted. Fran would put Pepsi on his pacifier and in his bottle. He wouldn't do anything without Pepsi and would scream and cry without it. As you'd expect, his teeth were very bad at a young age. Dad and Fran didn't seem to care. Nor did they seem to take care of Robby. That job fell on me.

I took care of Robby after Fran went to bed or even when she was awake. Fran stayed in bed drinking coffee and smoking. I loved Robby like he was my own little one; it was as if I was his mother. I taught him to read and write, his ABCs, and played with him with his Star Wars action figures. It hurt when I would step on those figures! They were scattered everywhere on the floor. Sometimes It seemed like they would be there forever unless I picked them up and threw them away. Looking back, I should have saved them. They would probably be worth something today for a Star Wars collector.

Fran had two daughters, Krista and Kay. They would come to visit every weekend. I enjoyed their visits most of the time. Krista spent a lot of time at her dad's, and I didn't spend much time with her. Maybe she was a loner or maybe she felt out of place when she was over at Fran and my dad's. I became very close with Kay. She was beautiful with long hair. She developed early which, for girls, means breasts before the other girls. She had big boobs which got a lot of attention from boys. I wanted to be like her. She was good at sports and forthright with what she was thinking. She said what she thought even if it would hurt someone's feelings. I wanted to do that, too; to be that self-confident and not have to worry about anyone's approval. I also didn't want to hurt someone else's feelings. Kay didn't seem to care whose feelings she hurt.

Whenever my stepmom would wake up, I knew it was time for me to bring her coffee. It wasn't morning because of her night job, but it was her morning. I felt like I was her servant. I tried so hard to do things right for her so that she would complement me or give me some sort of recognition, and even some sort of motherly love. But I don't remember many compliments. I didn't have my mother's love or the love and support of Fran, no matter how hard I tried to take care of both of them. I was a caregiver to everyone trying to get that love. I would watch my stepsister lie in bed with her mother Fran and they would talk and laugh together. I felt excluded when I would bring coffee or complete any other chore while they cuddled and tickled each other.

I couldn't turn to my dad for parental love and affection because of the sexual abuse. But I still wanted the love of a parent. He was usually out, maybe at the grocery store. Or maybe he would be visiting the neighbor that he was having sex with. It didn't matter. What I longed for was a mother. I wished to be loved by a mother like Kay was. I was usually cleaning, cooking, or helping Robbie. As I would get down on my hands and knees and clean the closets, I made things spotless. I would clean every spot and every piece of lint. I cleaned and worked so hard because I wanted Fran to be proud of me and give me some of that love that she gave her daughters.

I remember Christmas came and went a few times. It was everyone else's favorite time of the year, but not mine. Opening presents on Christmas morning was torture every year that I lived with my dad and stepmom. Every year dad and Fran would ask what we wanted. One Christmas, I told them I wanted a digital clock radio. Kay wanted one, too. We both wanted to have one next to our bed to listen to music, dance, and have fun together. And I wanted a pair of Levi jeans.

When Christmas morning came, I was wide awake because I was excited about getting a clock radio. We woke up Robby so that he would get Fran and dad up. I knew to never wake them. Kay and I made Robby wake them up because he never got in trouble. Robby always got to go first. He always had the most presents under the tree. Kay was next to open, and she had the most awesome clock radio. It was digital with the bright red numbers and speakers on it. I couldn't wait to open mine.

I waited and watched her open the rest of her presents, a couple of pairs of Levi jeans and some cool T-shirts to go with them. Levi's and T-shirts were the popular look in school. I was a cool kid, at least I thought I was, so I always wanted to dress cool. It was my turn to open up my presents, I would always open the biggest one last. I knew it had to be a good one. I opened the small ones first. When I saw my first gift, I opened it. It was a clock radio, but it wasn't like Kay's. It had numbers that flipped as the minutes and seconds and hours went by and the speakers were small. A lump grew in my throat. It felt like I want to just start crying. I held it in because I didn't want Fran to see me sad or disappointed. I wanted them to know I was grateful for what I got. I moved on to the other presents. I was ready for those Levi's. I opened my clothes package. I knew it was clothing because of the feel of the gift. I opened it up and it was the ugliest polyester stretch pants. I thought Fran must hate me. The lump in my throat grew larger. I kept calm and smiled. Fran asked me if I had a good Christmas. I said, "Oh yes, I did. Thank you". This pattern was repeated every Christmas.

It wasn't just at Christmas time that I felt that disappointment. That feeling that Kay was loved more and that Fran intentionally was trying to give me less than she gave her own daughter was an everyday feeling. My stepmom didn't let me grow hair long. She would always make me get it cut so short that my ears would be showing. I wanted to grow long beautiful hair like Kay's. I didn't show how sad I was. I just kept doing what she wanted me to do and never letting her know how I was hurting inside.

When Kay went back to her dad's house I was left there alone with Fran and dad. Kay was like my protector because she would tell her mom to stop being mean to me. Fran would always tell me and my brother Bobby and how worthless we were and how horrible our mother was. She would tell us we are ugly, and nobody would want us. I felt as if Bobby and I were the servants in the house. The story of Cinderella and the mean stepmother making her a servant was not a fairy tale in that house.

Bobby left for the military when he was 18. He was a couple of years older than me, and I didn't see him much, but the abuse that he got was just as bad as mine. At night when everyone was asleep my brother and I would sneak into the kitchen and get a piece of bread, roll it up in a ball and eat it. We were so hungry. Sometimes she just wouldn't let us eat. We even took my little brother's Pepsi 2 L bottle and drank some from it. It was so cold and so good.

Fran would beat us so badly. I always recovered from it on the outside but I still feel the pain of those beatings on the inside. I wouldn't cry. I would not let her see me cry. The mental abuse was always worse and took a long time to recover from. When someone tells you you're worthless and you're ugly and no one will ever love you or want you, you grow up thinking that way. Maybe Fran was right, and I deserved the treatment because I was unworthy of good things and happy things.

The abuse with my stepmother continued over and over every day. My stepmother doled out the physical and emotional abuse while my father was the source of the sexual abuse in that house. I woke up every day hoping I could get out of the house and leave.

When my daughter, Francheska, was about two months old, Fran said to me, "you need a break why don't you go out with some friends and have fun I will watch the baby for you." I wasn't sure whether to trust her. She usually wasn't nice to me, and it didn't make sense for her to offer to watch my baby. I wasn't sure what her angle was, but I decided to go out since Fran was offering. I got dressed up, put on makeup, and went out with a boy I met a few months ago. We had a good time watching TV and laughing and eating pizza. He brought me home about midnight. It felt good to get out and get away for a while.

Being a new mom was very tiring and I had a lot of pressure on me. I didn't get much sleep. I was new to this mom thing. I did my best with her when she was a baby. When I got home and walked into my bedroom, my stepmother yelled at me "where have you been, you whore? You worthless piece of shit. Where have you been?" I was shocked. Why was she so angry? She had offered for me to go out.

5

Family Feud

My mom Glenda and my dad Bob had two children together: my brother Bobby, Robert Thomas Whaley, Jr., and me, Dorothy Lynne Whaley. Before my mom married my dad, she had a daughter named Angela Renee Young. Young was my mother's maiden name.

After mom and dad's divorce dad got remarried a couple more times. Dad's second marriage was to a lady that I hardly remember, but they had a son. He was a red-headed, freckled-faced boy they named Eddie. Dad didn't visit Eddie much, nor pay child support for him. Fran and dad were married soon after dad's second marriage ended. They then had Robbie together. After he married Fran, she wouldn't allow dad to do anything for Eddie because she didn't want him to love any other child except Robbie. Robbie is now in his 40s and still acts like a spoiled brat.

Bobby

My brother Bobby was a little nerdy fella with a large nose. He broke that big nose playing football and got it fixed. After he got a new nose, all the girls loved him. They still do. He was born the same day I was but two years before. We were both born the day before Valentine's Day. Mom always told us she was putting Bobby's birthday cake in the oven when she went into labor with me. Bobby and I always shared a birthday cake when we were together at the same time, which we rarely were. After mom and dad divorced, Bobby went straight to live with my dad and I went to Grandma's. Bobby always sided with dad's side of the family and his love for dad was overwhelming. I understand the love of a son and a father. They did spend a lot of time together because, as I said, Bobby went with him at a very young age.

Bobby never cared much for mom. I guess it's because he never knew her, and he only listened to the views of other people—like dad and Fran—and they hated mom. They didn't like what she was doing and the way she was living her life. They always put her down and told us about it all the time. It would make me mad and sad because I love my mom. No matter what people say about a parent of yours, they are still your parent. I saw a lot of bad things happen to her so I felt sorry for her, even at an early age. Bobby never saw the stuff that I had with mom. He only heard the judgment coming from other people.

Bobby was raised to think he could always be better. I guess that is the word to use. Bobby's always been a hard worker and excelled in everything that he has done. He was in the military for a short spell and got out and got married. He had kids and got divorced. Then, got married and divorced again. Bobby and I always stayed close because it was just us. We shared the same two parents and we both thought that was very special. I stood up for

Bobby many times when he got bullied at school. I would beat up people that made fun of him for being such a nerdy little boy even though he was my big brother. It hurt me to see him suffer and be sad.

What hurt me the most was the way he was treated by Fran. Fran put him down and would hit him and tell him all kinds of mean things—the type of mean things that would stick in a person's mind for a lifetime and make them feel worthless about themselves. Bobby always held his head high and was a good speaker and a good listener. He talked a lot about himself as dad will talk about himself. They always bragged about this and that and how good they are at this and that. It's good when you're proud of yourself for something, but when you overdo it, it gets annoying. They overdid it at times.

My heart would break when Fran would slap Bobby in the head or the face. Or spit on him, as she did on me many times. That's a very disrespectful thing to do to somebody. Any abuse is disrespectful.

Bobby wasn't abused much as a young child. More physical abuse began as he became a preteen. Bobby is now 56 and not in good health. It may seem like he is because he talks big, but I know he's got some health issues. He's gained a lot of weight and been through a lot of ups and downs with relationships. He hasn't been very involved with me, Mom, Angie, and Amy. He's always been a loner.

We were considered part of a lower class, if you will, of people who use government assistance, have been in jail, argued, drank, did drugs, and so on and so on. Bobby would share this story with all of his family and friends in the future; the sad story about his horrible other side of the family that he is ashamed of. Oh, I'm sure he loved us in his way, but we were always the ones that were put on the back shelf with him. It's crazy because I loved him so much. I still do. Mom would cry a lot and want to talk to him, but he was never close with her and never came to see her, just a few times here and there. At her funeral, he cried and felt guilty because he wasn't there as much as he would've liked to have been. Maybe it was just guilty tears falling and talking because after the funeral was over it went back to the same. He lived his life, and we lived our life. I took care of mom and all her needs, and he takes care of dad and all of his needs.

It's hard to believe that someone we love so much, like a parent, could do something so terrible. Maybe we need for them to be good and someone to trust and look up to because we are their child. I told Bobby many times about what dad had done to me and he told me it was all in my head and I was making it up. Sometimes it seemed like he would believe me, but I knew down deep he didn't want to believe me. His dad or dad could do no wrong in his eyes. And that's OK for him to feel that way. Everybody is entitled to think and believe what they want. When you tell the truth to someone and they don't believe you it's OK because you know what the truth is.

I tell Bobby all the time to come on up and I'll make sure he has a nice bed to sleep in, dinner and a couple of drinks, and some good times. He never takes me up on my offer but that's OK. One day he'll be crying over me if I pass before he does. And his tears of guilt and wishing he would've gotten to spend more time with me will spill down his face like they did when mom passed.

Amy

I had two sisters, Angie and Amy; Angie was four years older than me, and Amy was six years younger.

What a silly, crazy, funny girl Amy was. When she was little and when she became an adult, she was the life of the party. She lived with grandma from birth. She never knew her dad and was never really close with her mom because Grandma Margret was essentially her mom. Angie always came first, and Amy knew it. Amy was always on the back burner. Amy was a little nerdy. She couldn't do anything except go to church and out to eat with grandma. Amy was a chunky girl growing up. People made fun of her and that hurt her feelings. I always felt bad for her and tried to be her friend. I tried to talk to her and thought we were close. At least we tried to be, as much as possible.

When Amy got old enough to leave Grandma Margaret's house she went crazy. At age 20 something, she moved out. She did all the things she should've done as a teenager. Amy was a little backward. When she was younger, she grew up completely differently. When she was an adult she had the balls to tell people what she felt about everything. She didn't worry about hurting anyone's feelings. She would tell me, "Dottie, you need to stop letting people run over you. And quit being so damn nice." I couldn't help it. It was me.

I always wanted Amy to come over and stay with me. To talk and laugh because she cracked everybody up. She would have the best jokes and act so silly until we were all crying with laughter.

Times weren't always fun with her, but I always loved her. She was my little sister and I always had to make sure she was OK. Amy didn't grow up in a normal, happy family either. But she grew up in the most normal family we had in our family tree. She would tell me many times about grandpa Henri molesting her. Grandma Margret didn't believe her when she told her, but I did because he would molest me when grandma went to church and I stayed behind. I guess, I kind of got used to it. I stopped telling everybody what happened when I was molested. It's a shame nobody believed me or would listen to me, but life goes on.

Amy made some poor choices as an adult. She made a poor choice in men. She didn't keep a job for long. She had a lot of health issues. She had two children, Calah and Dakota. Both were beautiful, strong, independent kids. Calah came to live with me for a couple of years while she was in high school. I took care of her like she was my own, as I did everybody else that needed a place to stay. I would get her Christmas presents as I would buy them for my own. I would help Amy often with things she needed in life. It wasn't a lot that I helped her with. It was $20 here. $20 there. It was whatever I could afford at the time of her need.

Amy was married a couple of times. Her last husband was Mike. I didn't care much for Mike, Mike wasn't her soulmate; she didn't even like him. He was lazy and didn't care about anything except smoking his pot and playing pool. There's nothing wrong with either of them but if you don't have a job why do it? But who am I to judge?

Mike and Amy got into a wreck on the highway going to the interstate. A state police officer T-boned them. Amy got a settlement and bought a house of her own for them to live in. She paid cash. She put the house in her name only. I asked her why and she said because she wanted to make sure her grandchildren had something from her that she could pass on. I thought that was a good idea. She didn't want to put it in Mike's name because she didn't want him to have anything. After all, he never did anything to help, except make her feel worthless.

I think Amy might've been envious of me for the choices I made in life. I was the one that worked and took care of my bills and when I had extra I would fix my house up. It wasn't always new because I loved yard sales. I would find good deals. It seemed like Amy would always think poorly of me for the things I had. I worked for it and it was as if I were the bad person. Amy and my other sister Angie would talk about me. I got used to it over time. I was just like them, no different. However, I made very different choices.

Angie

My sister Angie was a crazy gal from the beginning. She was a beautiful girl; tiny, long blonde hair, blue eyes, and dimples. Gorgeous. She was raised by my mom's mom, grandma Margret, and her husband Henry. Mom had Angie at an early age. So, as I discussed in a previous chapter, they grew up together so Angie seems more like an aunt than a sister.

When Angie became a young teenager, she got into all kinds of trouble and always hung with the wrong people. She got pregnant at the age of 14 and had Brandy. Brandy was a beautiful baby. She became a beautiful adult and now has five children of her own and many grandchildren.

Angie was married quite a few times. I think she might have beaten the family record. She was probably married six times. Her first husband, Jesse, was in a motorcycle gang. He was a cool guy. (His younger brother Fritzie was the first boy I ever kissed. We French-kissed and I didn't know what I was doing, of course, but apparently, I did OK because we kissed a second time later.) I would hang with Angie many times when she would let me. She was always out with her friends drinking, partying, and having a good time. She was the life of the party because of her personality and her looks. She was smart, too. She wasn't afraid to speak her mind, and I wish I had inherited that trait too.

Angie's second husband was named George and he was a very mean, evil man. He was the devil. He beat her all the time, and not just with his fist. He would hit her with bricks, bottles, brooms, rocks, whatever he could find until she would end up in a hospital, lifeless. He was a mean, short man with no teeth. He was a horrible bully of a monster. He even broke my grandmother's legs while she was sitting at the table with her feet propped up. He broke her legs with my sister's son's highchair. It would all begin with a couple of drinks and laughs and then it would turn into a nightmare at the end of the night. We always knew what was going to happen soon as the first beer was cracked open.

I took the bus one night to visit Angie and spend the night. She always thought that I suspected I was better than anybody because I lived with my dad. In her and my mom's minds, they thought they were the Beaver Cleaver parents and we always had what we wanted. Not true. Not true at all. After the bus dropped me off a few blocks from her house I walked up and went in as she was frying chicken. Angie was the best cook ever. She always told me a little hint on how to do her fried chicken. I always remember that little hint when I fry my chicken to this day.

George and a few other of his brothers were there. It was a very hot summer day and family was in and out pretty much all day long. After dinner, they cracked open the drinks. I didn't drink—I mean I did at times here and there, but I was never into it. It just wasn't for me. I was sitting on the couch a couple of hours later when I heard screaming and hollering. Angie came running from the kitchen with a towel around her head, soaked in blood. She was screaming, "Help me! Help me!" I didn't know what to do. I was scared, but I ran after my sister. Outside, she fell to the ground and could hardly talk; she was so scared. Blood was everywhere. I had never seen so much blood in my life. I went over and I laid on top of her and held her. I said, "everything's going to be OK. I got you! I won't let nothing happen to you."

Her husband George came running out shortly after and I was still on top of her holding her. I was pressing the towel against where he had beat her in the head with a cinder block. He told me to get up off of her now or he would kill me. I raised my head while still holding my sister's towel to her head to stop the bleeding. I looked him right in the eye and said, "You will have to kill me first." I guess God and His angels were on my side because he just walked away. I don't know what came over me that night. Maybe I was just stupid or maybe I just loved Angie enough for me to get hurt instead of her.

I remember calling my grandmother to come and get her. We went to the hospital where she stayed for a couple of days. When she got out grandma bought her new furniture for her new apartment to get away from George: new cars, new dishes, new furniture, a new washer and dryer—everything she needed to start all over again. But this didn't happen just one time. This was a pattern that was repeated many times. My grandmother would buy Angie a new house. She would buy mini cars for my sister, Angie, just for her to wreck them or for her husband to wreck them… or to sell them for drugs.

I always worried about Angie. I called her my angel many times when I was a baby. She loved me calling her that. She would take me skating a lot with her. Well, actually, she would drop me off at the skating rink and go with her friends to do what teenagers did together. I would be having fun at the skating rink, dancing, eating popcorn, drinking pop, and having a good time enjoying life. I remember dancing to *Kung Fu Fighting*. Angie would finally come in before the rink closed and dance with me to that song. She was a great dancer. I guess she learned it from my mom. Angie was a stripper, too, for a while. I guess if I had a good body, I would've been one. But then again, No, I wouldn't have because I'm too shy.

Angie and Mom moved back and forth to Covington, Kentucky from Tell City, Indiana every time the weather would change into a nice spring day. They would go up north and get an apartment and lose what they had in Tell City. When the weather would get cold and nothing to do out on the streets, they would come back to Tell City. Grandma would always fix Angie up with something nice.

Meanwhile, I worked four jobs taking care of four kids and struggling every second. Grandma Margret would stop by many times outside my house with my sister Angie in the car. I'd say, "Grandma, do you have five dollars I could borrow until I get my check?" She would take her big, gigantic purse and put her hand down in the bottom, and shake it for all the loose change she could find in one swoop. She would say, "Here you go." I would say, "No, thank you. I'll be all right". After she would leave, she would take Angie and her kids out to eat somewhere and buy them new clothes, new shoes, whatever they wanted. She would take care of every need and anything that they wanted. It made me so mad, but I was really glad somebody was helping her out. She did have two children and I love them dearly.

Mom and Angie would get in trouble a lot and be in jail for stealing, robbing somebody, drugs, and what have you. Angie was in jail a lot for drinking and driving and different things. I was always so worried about her driving. She even drove on the wrong side of the highway and I'm so thankful that no one was hurt. Grandma asked me to go with her to drive wherever Angie was in jail so I could drive them back home. Grandma couldn't see too well so I was the driver and I went every time.

Mom and Angie also bought a lot of drugs. At the bars in town, mom and Angie were a team. They would meet men and pretend to want to go somewhere private with them. Then they would steal their wallet and everything that was in it to buy drugs.

They talked me into going to the doctor one day, because I was a little chunky, and asking the doctor for diet pills. I didn't think much of it. They were both a little heavy at that time, so I realized what was going on. I went to the doctor and got the medicine for them. I may have seemed stupid sometimes, but I kept everything up in my head and my mind, and my memory. I wasn't stupid; I was very smart.

Angie and I had a love-hate relationship, and I was OK with that. One time, Angie gave me a VCR which she stole later from me. I got mad at her so many times for the things she did and the people she hurt. I didn't stay mad, though. That anger went away each time we had our sister talk. She babysat a lot for me because I needed the help. My kids were there pretty much all of the time. They were young and I worked so many jobs I didn't know if I was coming or going. I would pay her with the food stamps I was receiving so that her kids would always have food. I gave her cash, as well. I signed up for some assistance to get childcare help. The government would help pay for the person babysitting your children. Eventually, she would get mad at me and wouldn't babysit anymore. But she still kept the money that the government was paying her to watch my children.

Although I loved her, I was very scared of Angie. She intimidated me to no end. She had a mean side to her, and I didn't want to get on that mean side. When we would argue she would bring up everything that I ever did wrong. I hated that. I think she did it as a way to get away from the conversation at hand. Others have used that tactic on me, too. They would use it as a way to turn the situation around so that I would feel guilty for something, and the argument would end. Because I never wanted to argue, I always just walked away like a dog with its tail between its legs. I didn't want to fight; I saw too much of it growing up. I saw my mom get beaten by many men. I saw her get raped by men. I saw my sister beaten by her husband and boyfriends. My anxiety would go crazy whenever anybody would start an argument or fight around me. It always scared me like when I was little and I heard the loud sirens coming from the police or ambulance while I was playing in that park behind my babysitter's house. I wanted to go hide. I was scared to hear that because I knew something bad is happening to someone I loved.

Angie and I only got into one physical fight in our life. I don't even remember what it was about but she pulled out a big chunk of my hair, and then she bit me on the arm. I will never forget it. Angie would get into fights every time she was drinking. The family always knew what was going to happen. So, when the time came and when that part of Angie came out, we all left and went home from where we were. We didn't want to be involved in any trouble. Sometimes my younger sister Amy and I would call the police on her if we knew she was drinking and driving just so she would go to jail and not hurt anybody or herself. She never knew this but I'm sure if she had known, she probably would have killed us. Bahahaha. Her drug habit and drinking were really serious. When Angie was good, she was the best Angie. When she was drinking and doing drugs, it wasn't good at all. It never ever turned out well.

6

You are My Sunshine

The pain of childbirth is the kind of pain that you never forget. I didn't have long labor with my first child, but I remember the pain. Every moan was worth it when I saw Francheska (Ches) for the first time. I nicknamed her Ches, just like the game, but now I wish that I hadn't, because Francheska is such a beautiful name. I was barely 17 when I delivered her at a hospital in Covington, Kentucky.

Ches had the longest, darkest, most beautiful hair ever. I dressed her in bows and a beautiful little purple outfit when I took her home from the hospital. She was born on Super Bowl Sunday, January 22nd, 1984. My stepmother thought that she might have been a mixed baby of some kind: half Mexican, African-American, or Native-American. I don't know because I wasn't sure who her father was. Not knowing that major detail haunted me for a long time.

My baby and I settled in my little bedroom at my dad and Fran's house. It was a small two-bedroom apartment. I had her little bassinet beside me so I could hear every little word she made. She was the most beautiful baby I'd ever seen in my life, and she was also my first real love. Ches was the first person who would love me forever, and I would love her back exactly the same.

Being a new mom was overwhelming. I was tired all the time from lack of sleep and went through all of those emotions that I couldn't even understand or explain. When Ches was two- or three-months-old Fran told me that I needed to go out with my friends. Being a new mom was overwhelming. I went out with my friends and met up with one of my old boyfriends. I went out and had a good time.

As I mentioned in an earlier chapter, my stepmother saw me and started calling me all sorts of names. A *****. worthless person, horrible mother, piece of ****. I was so mad. I was hurt. How dare she call me all these names after I've done everything for her? I slaved for her. I cleaned up every part of this apartment and let the man next to her do things to me. Things that he wasn't supposed to do. He was my dad.

I don't know what came over me at that moment, but I looked her in the eye, held up my hand with my finger, and pointed straight at my dad. I said, "If I'm a ******* *****, it's because of that man right there!"

Fran said, "What do you mean? What are you talking about?"

I said, "Tell her, Dad, tell her." Of course, he looked at me like he didn't know what I was talking about. It was as if I made it all up. Lies. My stepmom took me by the hair of my head and threw me onto the bed where my dad was laying. She said "You want him? You ******* Now, he's yours." That's not what a child wants to hear. I may have been a mother at a young age with a new baby, but I was still a child. And what had happened to me as a child, nobody believed me when I told them.

It was very devastating to not be believed. My father had done things to me—molested me—and no one believed me. I told my stepmom to ask my sister, Kay. "Ask her, she will tell you the truth. She won't lie to you. She will tell you. Go ask her." My stepmom called Kay on the phone and asked. Kay was of course scared and intimidated by her mom. She, also, didn't want to hurt my dad's feelings. FUCK his feelings. Did he have feelings when he was abusing us, taking our innocence away? Taking it took a part of us away that would hinder our life forever. No. He didn't feel sorry for us.

When Francheska was born I made a promise to her that I would not let anything happen to her. I promised that I would give her the love that I never had or felt and I would protect her every day of her life. But I felt like I had already failed the promises that I made to Ches when she was born. So, I packed mine and my daughter's clothes as best I could in a couple of trash bags. I took Ches's baby bed apart and sat outside on the front curb of that apartment. I sat on that curb for about 4 hours with my baby, Francheska. She slept; I cried. What was I gonna do?

I waited for my grandmother, Margaret, to come and pick me up from the curb outside my dad's apartment. When she got there, her car was a mess as always. It was full of leftover food. There were chicken nuggets, pizza boxes, donuts, a couple of 2-liter bottles of water, and all sorts of left-over trash. She had uncontrolled diabetes and she didn't care what she ate. I knew there was a good meal leftover in the seat somewhere. I managed to put all my stuff in her car, and we drove the three hours to my grandma's home. I stayed with her for about a week, my baby and me. She signed me up for some housing that went by my income, and I got food stamps and applied for welfare.

My first apartment came through government-assisted housing. When I went to hook up the utilities on the apartment, they asked me if it was electric or gas. I told them it had plugins because I didn't know what they meant. I just thought everything was electric and you put gas in a car. I've learned a lot since.

We lived in our little one-bedroom apartment for a couple of years. I worked at the courthouse cleaning for the judge and cleaning some of the other offices that were there. I enjoyed cleaning because I enjoyed making things better.. I'd pick up other odd jobs, babysitting or cleaning for this person, or caring for that person, doing whatever I could to make sure my daughter had what she needed.

But I didn't always make good choices. Sometimes I worked jobs that I needed to get her diapers and sometimes I had to do other things that I didn't want to do to get Francheska her diapers. After all, it is what I knew best in life from such an early age.

Ches was growing up so fast right before my eyes. She was so beautiful. So funny. She loved me so much and I loved her. She had long beautiful dark hair, beautiful eyes, and a beautiful smile. I was so proud. I always made sure she had clean clothes for school, and I brushed and curled her hair. I always tried to do my best to give her what I could.

When Ches was about five or six, I bought my first house. I was so excited. So happy so proud. It was a five-bedroom house on three levels. It was only $19,000, and a friend of mine had completely renovated it. My friend lived there still, and I allowed him and his other roommates to rent from me. It was a great way to make some extra money to get by. It was also fun.

I started working as a bartender in town at a place called the Swiss House. It was an awesome place with awesome people that worked there like my good friend, Holly, who I loved dearly. She would always put her change on the counter. I'm sure it was probably about $40 worth of change. Every night I would try to tell her to pick it up. Eventually, I'd pick it up. Every night she let me have the change. There was a lip on the bar which made the change hard to pick up, but I didn't mind.

The Swiss House had bands that would come and play which brought people from all over to come to hear the live music. It was a nice place to hang out and meet people. It was awesome. Looking back, I felt like that was a pretty good time of my life.

I met a guy in a band. His name was Andy. Or was it? Anyways, it was a two-man band, and he was nice. We got together for about a month or more while he played at the Swiss House. He was a really good-looking guy. He told me about his history, his family, and how he got started playing music. He told me about how he was adopted and about where he was from. I liked him a lot even though I knew it wasn't going to last. I knew it wasn't serious, but I enjoyed my time with him.

While I was seeing Andy, I liked this other man named David. He was so cute. We were into each other, and I really liked him a lot. He lived in Owensboro, which was probably over 30 minutes from where I lived. We saw each other a little bit here and there, off and on. I liked him more than he liked me. At some point, I found out he had a girlfriend.

I went to my sister, Angie's House sat on her bed, and cried because I was pregnant. Angie was excited for me, but I told her that I would never be able to love a second child as much as I love Francheska. I couldn't imagine loving anyone else that much. How can that be done? How could you love another child after you're so in love with a child already? She said it was OK, it will all come together. It will all fall into place. You'll love this baby as much as you love Ches. I told her that I couldn't see how that could happen.

I told David that he was the father many times; however, he didn't believe me. I told him not to worry, or whatever, I could take care of the baby on my own. Of course, I could. I did with my first one. I always thought Francheska's father was a man I met while visiting my mother for spring break. He was a pig farmer. But then again, it could be the man who raped me at my mom's apartment while I was visiting her during spring break. I always felt guilty for Ches not having a father in her life, and it appeared my second child wouldn't have a father, either.

Brittany

Brittany was born on August 28, 1989. I remember going into labor with her. I was sitting on my living room floor and Francheska was about five years old, and I was pulling lice eggs out of her hair. Ches had the thickest, most beautiful hair, and, for some reason every year, she would always contract lice while being in school. At first, it was embarrassing that she got lice, but I got used to it. I sat there for hours, bent over trying to make sure I got every little bit out that was in her hair. As the hours went by my stomach started hurting. I had some cramps, and I hoped this might be the day for Brittany to make her arrival so I went to the hospital.

After being checked, the doctor told me I wasn't ready yet to go into full labor. The nurse said to walk around while out in the parking lot. So, I did. Finally, the time came and she was ready to be welcomed into the world. Her doctor was nowhere to be found. So, another doctor who was just coming in to check some messages was on call so he was tasked with my delivery. My labor went so fast that he still had his golf shirt on. They quickly put a gown on him, and it was time for Brittany to come.

Brittany was a beautiful, chunky baby. She was a good baby, too. After bringing Brittany home, it was so nice to have Francheska there to help me with her. And my sister was right… I would be able to love another child. I love both my girls very much. They are my world. Just like with Francheska, I promised Brittany that I would love her as best as I could and give her the life I never had: a life of love, security, and protection. Just as with Francheska, that would turn out to be another broken promise.

After Brittany was born, I felt my mind slipping into a dark place. I would try to sleep and my mind wouldn't shut down. I would hear a voice or a thought that would keep telling me I needed to kill Ches. I didn't want to tell anyone because I didn't want people to think I was crazy, or have the welfare take my kids away from me. I kept fighting the voices in my mind. The voice said to get a knife and stab her. I yelled at the voice and told the voice no!! I'd pray "God, please help me, make it stop." I got rid of the knives in the kitchen. I knew I had to keep fighting the voice. This went on for about two years. Every night was a nightmare for me to fight. Later, I would find out through my shrink that the voice was bad. It tried to get to me and take over. I knew it was a voice of *something*, but I fought, and I won! In a way, I won. This happened years before anyone talked about postpartum depression. I would never want to hurt my kids... ever! I know now that God was watching over me and my babies.

Brittany was very possessive of me. She wouldn't let me out of her sight. She cried if I went to the restroom; she cried if I had to go to the store or anything. Going to work was a chore every day because she cried her little eyes out constantly. If I had a boyfriend and she saw me hold hands with him, she would throw a fit and scream and cry and take his hand off of mine and put her hand in my hand.

I finally got a hold of Brittany's father, David. It was a little complicated at first getting things started for her to visit her father, but everything went well. He was a very good dad and had a wonderful family. He paid $30 a week in child support, and I was grateful for anything.

When Brittany was in her early teens, I decided to have a paternity test to give us all 100% peace of mind. I wasn't prepared for the results. The DNA test showed that David was not her biological father. Brittany was really, really hurt. I was as well. But it didn't seem to bother David. He didn't seem hurt at all. Instead, he just stopped everything. No more child support. No more visits. No more calls. No more anything.

I still carry that guilt.

7

Nightmares

As I was enjoying my new little family, I didn't realize that the worst chapter in my life was coming. I knew I was missing out on something in my life, and I guess that was love. I desperately wanted somebody to love me and take care of me.

In 1989, I met a man named James. A friend fixed me up with James, even though he was in prison at the time. When we started talking on the phone, I was pregnant with my daughter, Brittany. After months of talking to James on the phone, I went to visit him. When I met him initially, I thought he was the ugliest man I'd ever laid eyes on. He had long hair, a goatee, and a mustache. He had the darkest, deep brown eyes I'd ever seen. I didn't know the devil lay behind those eyes.

When James was released, I picked him up from prison up north of Indiana. It was a bitterly cold day. I was kind of scared in a way, yet kind of happy to have him finally in my life. I was tired of taking care of myself emotionally and needed somebody stronger than me to help. He seemed to fit everything that I thought I needed. I've made a lot of mistakes, but this was the biggest of my life.

The week before James gave me a list of items he asked me to bring: a gun, a bag of weed, a 5th of Beam, 7-year-old whiskey, and clothes and shoes. This seems crazy to me in retrospect, but I needed to show my love for him. James had a voice that was very deep and very strong. I mistakenly thought he would be the protector and take care of me and my children. So, I did the things that he asked. I needed him to love me so that he would keep me safe from anything that would ever hurt me again. I needed that protection that it felt like he was offering. That's the kind of love I wanted.

I lived 7 hours away from the correctional facility at the top of Indiana. I had never even visited a jail before. I certainly had never bought a bag of weed before. Yes, smoked a joint or two with people but not bought a bag.

After many hours of driving, I pulled through the guard shack. The guard asks, "Ma'am, would you like to declare anything drugs, gun, etc.?" I panicked. I don't know what else he said. I'm like, Oh no. What have I gotten myself into? I was scared.

So, I told the lady, "Look. Here's the deal. I've got a gun in the car. I'm picking up a man I just met, and I want to make sure I'm safe." Right off the bat, I started lying for James. The guard told me that I needed to take that gun back to my room or wherever I'm staying. I told her that I would be right back, and I took the weed and the gun to the motel that I was staying at. What in the hell was I thinking? I wasn't because he made my thinking disappear. He was thinking for me.

After walking out of the prison, James got in my car. We went to a local restaurant close to where he was incarcerated, and he took his clothes and went to the restroom to change. He was gone 45 minutes. This was way too long to just change clothes. I started to worry that he had just left me here. And that he had run out the back door with his stuff. I was relieved when he finally came out of the bathroom. I didn't ask him why he took 45 minutes. I knew not to question him. We just sat down to eat like nothing was wrong. I just accepted his behavior. Then we went back to my motel room and had sex for the first time.

After lunch, we headed to eastern Kentucky because he wanted to make a stop in Paintsville. It was his ex-wife's house where his son lived. I was waiting in the car for quite a while, probably about 3 hours. I was OK with that because I knew he had to have missed his son. I found out later that he was in there having sex with his ex-wife while I waited out in the car. I was thinking of all the fun things we were going to do as a family. I was so stupid. So gullible. I still feel the painful embarrassment of how stupid I was to believe him and just wait outside for that long. I should be feeling, what kind of man does this to me? After many years of this happening with men and other women, I guess I got used to it.

After the stop at his ex-wife's house, we went on to meet his family. They were all coal miners and they all had names that rhymed. I thought they seemed nice. His mom loved to cook, and the family loved to eat. And they sure loved their brother, James.

After all the visits, we traveled back to Tell City, IN. During the 4-1/2 hour drive, I got to listen to his deep voice, his ways of talking and moving his body, and the sound that he makes. I watched and listened to all the new things that I didn't get a chance to see while he was incarcerated. Everything was new to each other. We got home and settled in.

Somewhere between the time he was released from prison and the way home, I got pregnant with my third daughter. Her name is Shy 'Leah. Shy for short. I didn't know I was pregnant for a few weeks after we got back to my house. Things seemed to be going OK for a week or two. Being in prison for seven years, I'm sure things were different for him. I was still in love with this man.

I started to feel like my mind was losing control. I let go of all of my independence. It was as if I was a walking zombie because he controlled my mind. When I first found out I was pregnant he said, "everything is going to be OK. Everything's gonna be OK, I'll take care of it, Dorothy" in his deep, evil voice.

After a few months of living together at my house, James decided he wanted to go live near his family. I felt like we should wait a while to, you know, see what happens. I didn't want to move right away. Maybe I did have a little sense about myself.

Months after his release, James was arrested for selling drugs to inmates. It was a prison drug bust and he had helped get the drugs inside the prison. James didn't have a real job or honest work. He made money selling drugs. James would go back to jail several times. I worked hard every day to support him and still thought he was the love of my life. I worshiped the ground that he walked on. I guess it was kind of a control thing on my part.

During this time, I was taking care of an elderly couple about 20-30 minutes from our house. They were a wonderful, loving couple who had met at a pie social many years ago and always held hands when they went to bed and fell asleep. That's what I wanted. I dreamed of having a love like that. Unfortunately, they were at the end of their days in life. I worked for them for about three months.

Because I had to have emergency Gallbladder surgery while I was there taking care of them, my younger sister Amy would care for them throughout the week. My best friend since I was 18 years old, Tina, would also help me on weekends.

When I returned to working for this couple after the surgery, I discovered that James was at our house having sex with my sister Amy. I found different types of my sister's clothes in the bedroom where they should not have been. I confronted her and I told her off. I destroyed her apartment the first time that I found out that they had sex. Amy was young. I was still mad at her, but I do not hold her responsible.

Even though James was doing these things, I still took him back. Later, they would still have sex together without me knowing. I caught them in a motel room. But I still loved him. Oh, I still loved him because he loved me. He told me he did. To any normal person, that should have been the last time for this to happen. But I wasn't in my right mind; I was under James's control.

Oprah

To my surprise, The Oprah Winfrey Show called me because the producers were planning a show about falling in love with men behind bars and wanted to interview me. I came to discover that my sister Amy had called the show.

Even though I was so pregnant at the time, I was on a mission to let the world know that I had found a good man behind bars. My best friend Tina, my sister Amy, and I went to the show together. My mom and her husband joined via satellite from the County jail (they both served a year or two for theft.) I planned to stand up for my man because my man loved me, and there was nothing wrong with falling in love with a man from prison. Even then I believed that James was going to take care of me and my whole family.

I had never been on a plane before. The show flew us to Chicago, and it was a hell of a trip, to say the least. When we were boarding the plane, I stopped right before you get on, right where the flight attendants greet you and put my hands on the plane while a crowd formed behind me. I prayed for our safety and safe travels. The people waiting behind me that day owe me a big "Thank you!".

The day we arrived Oprah's people put us up in a very nice hotel. We were so amazed by all of the cool things and nice stuff in the hotel. We were country girls that never ventured out of town, and I had definitely never stayed in a place that fancy. Later that evening we all went to eat at the snazzy restaurant downstairs in the hotel. We sat by a window and had a great view of downtown Chicago. We saw a bunch of different things that day out the window.

The big city was very different from the little town we came from—we only had three stop lights in our town.

Amy was the clown of us three. She always had us laughing and cracking up. I still loved my sister, even with what happened between her and James. On the elevator heading down to dinner that night, I made it clear that she had better not say a thing about that on the show. I told her in the meanest voice I could muster.

When we sat down for dinner, a nice man came over with a towel laid over his arm. He didn't talk to us; he just poured our water and stood right there next to our table. We wondered why he just stood there waiting. *We can't drink our water that fast*, we were thinking even though we didn't say it out loud.

When we placed our order, Amy decided to get an appetizer and selected raw oysters. Yuck! They brought the oysters out to us on a nice plate. I said, "Well, you going to eat that for real?" She said that she had never tried them before and wanted to.

Then Amy looked at the waiter and said "Hey, you know oysters make you horny. What are you doing later?" I couldn't believe she said that! I was so embarrassed, but I was also used to Amy's jokes. She would tell me all the time, "Dottie you have more issues than Playboy magazine." We all laughed and I ordered chicken. You never can go wrong with ordering chicken.

The producers of the show called us later that night and told us what time to meet the limo in the morning. A limo? She also said not to wear makeup or fix your hair. They would take care of that. So, we woke up, showered, and off we went like rock stars to get our hair and makeup fixed.

During our makeover, a man came in and told our makeup lady that she forgot her purse in his room. He was the star of the movie "Backlash." I can't remember his name, but he was going to be on after our show.

With our hair and makeup, all done, we left the green room to walk onto the stage. OMG! Here we are on the Oprah show! We felt like movie stars. Tina was disappointed that she didn't have her makeup or hair done up since she was to be part of the audience. But in the end, her interview was part of the show because they asked her questions and her thoughts.

While we waited for the famous Oprah to come out, we had the opportunity to see how they started a show. Some people worked there, and their job was to prep the audience. They were taught how to clap when Oprah would come out. They had to yell and scream and lots of stuff that you just don't think about.

Here comes OPRAH! I was a nervous wreck. It was hot up on the stage and I was pregnant which started making me feel sick to my stomach. Oprah came over to us and said "hello" and shook our hands. Then it was show time. There was a lady there that tried to plan an escape for her man behind bars. They used her story for a few episodes of "All My Children." where Erica tried to plan her man's break from prison. This story was based on this person's story on Oprah. It was a true story.

We were asked questions off and on. During a break for commercials, we had our makeup artists come and touch up our makeup. The commercial break was over. When

Amy was asked questions, she would freeze up and she couldn't talk. I had to finish what she wanted to say. Amy could say the boldest things to a waiter but froze on stage while being asked questions.

The audience was against us all. They thought it was wrong to have a relationship with anyone in jail. They were right but I didn't know it at the time. I fought for the love of my life right there on TV. Everyone in the world could see how stupid I was. Of course, at the time, I didn't think that. Finally, mom and her husband popped up on a big TV on stage. Mom told how her life was because of meeting the love of her life. She talked and said things, but it didn't matter because the world could see that they were in jail together. It didn't matter what they said because it was ridiculous to the audience and all the viewing world. Then it was Tina's time to speak her mind. Tina said she didn't think it was a good idea at all. Well, I was surprised. That's not what she had told me. Fate has a funny way of changing things because she later met a man behind bars while he was locked up, too.

The show was over and our star life ended. We went to the airport to fly back home. Before I got on the plane, I prayed again. Tina and Amy were plus-sized girls, so we all didn't fit together in a row. Amy and Tina sat in a row together with an empty seat between them and I had to sit in a row alone.

As our plane ascended, all hell broke loose. I had only flown on a plane once.

The pilot said to please put your seat belts on and remain calm. Which caused me to panic. WHAT?! I'm going to die alone! I started to pray and hold my stomach. I prayed for us all to make it. I prayed that, if we didn't make it, God would take care of my kids and watch over them. I asked one of the airline attendants to please sit next to me and pray with me. She did. We held hands and prayed together. We went through about an hour of bad weather, and we made it. I was never so happy to be on the ground. That experience didn't prevent me from flying again, even though I was so scared.

After being on the show, the embarrassment hit me. Why did I do that? Oh, my God. I am so stupid. I look like a fool.

But my nightmares didn't end there.

8

Jailhouse Rock

When I was six months pregnant with Shy, there was a knock at my front door. An officer asked, "are you Dottie May?" When I responded yes, he placed me under arrest! I didn't know what was going on when he took me in his patrol car.

He said I needed to come down to the station. I assumed that James had done something again that brought the cops here to question me. He said, "Well, it's not him. It's you. You're under arrest."

I was shocked. He told me I was under arrest for welfare fraud.

I said, "wait a minute, wait a minute." My kids were at a neighbor's house playing with a friend. I didn't have anyone to watch them. What was I gonna do? The cop told me to call someone as soon as possible or they would be taken to social services. I didn't know who to trust. My mom was in jail. My sister Angie was in prison at the time. I called Tina to come and keep them.

I went to the police station, and they were yelling at me in a room. "Dorothy, did you do this? Did you work for this couple in Huntingburg?"

I answered honestly, "yes, sir, I did."

"Dorothy, did you make this amount of money once a week?"

"Yes, sir, I did."

"Dorothy, did you collect food stamps while making this money?"

"Yes, sir, I did."

"Dorothy, did you use insurance money from the State of Indiana for the sum of $5000?"

"Yes, sir, I did. I had emergency gallbladder surgery."

"Dorothy, you are under arrest for welfare fraud."

I remember thinking, *wait a minute. I just told the truth. Why am I going to jail?* They were telling me I was facing 25 years to 50 in prison! I know I did wrong, but since I knew the reason why I did it, in my mind it was OK. I thought that if I told the truth they would understand and not place me under arrest.

The truth was, I received food stamps and $198 per month—the cash benefits of the elderly couple I cared for before they died—from government assistance. I didn't turn in my job of caring for these people, because I was desperate and wanted to make sure my children were taken care of. James was taking everything from me—every penny I had. This was Welfare Fraud.

My bond was set at $1,000. I'd never been in jail before. I didn't know what to do or say. I was so scared to be away for my children for even one day of their life, let alone to sit in jail. I waited for seven days for somebody to get me out.

Those couple days after I got out of jail were so scary. All I could think about is my children. I needed to find someone to watch my little ones so that they don't go to foster care. I called one of my friends to come and watch them until I could figure out something else and find out what was going on.

For the next couple of weeks, I was so paranoid. I remember hearing ambulances and police go by and becoming very scared. My anxiety from childhood had come back from when I was terrified that something had happened to my mom. Those sounds triggered fears of my mom being hurt. This time I was scared for myself.

When I would hear an ambulance or siren go off, I would take my children and run to the back of the house and hide in the bushes. I had them sit in the bushes for a long time. I know they were scared. It was like I was in a different world. My brain wasn't thinking right because I was so scared of losing my children. I was afraid of them being without me to protect them. I would do this many times, running to hide when I heard a siren. . My oldest daughter, would say, "Mom, what are we doing?" I said, "Shhh, don't say nothing". I bet we stayed there for an hour or two just waiting for the paranoia and anxiety to stop. It never left. It always stayed there. Just like it did when I was little.

My case went to trial when I was six-and-a-half months pregnant. The judge sentenced me to 25 years in prison! I was sick to my stomach. I remember thinking that I can't live without my children, and I don't want my children to live without me. Again, my brain wasn't thinking right. This took me back to after Brittany was born and I had heard the voices in my head. I think that's when a part of me began to crumble.

During all this craziness, James asked me to marry him. Of course, I said yes. He was in jail and I was nearly nine months pregnant and facing a prison sentence.

I dressed up as much as I could. A friend of mine and my grandma Margaret took me to the courthouse. James came into the courtroom in his prison jumpsuit and shackles and chains. I was wearing a pair of maternity pants and the biggest white shirt that I could find. I was ready huge and. I was miserable. But still, I was happy. It was the happiest day of my life. At least, I thought it would be.

A couple of days after I was married, I had my daughter Shy'leah in [month] of 1990. It was one of the hardest labors I ever had to go through, but I would not trade it for anything because she is a special beautiful, little girl. She was perfect—just like my other two. I called her Shy. It suited her since she was a shy baby. Even though I was still facing charges of welfare fraud and was very scared of the unknown, I knew my Shy was something very special.

The officer in charge of my case told me that if I could pay back the $5,000 that I had received in welfare benefits, I wouldn't have to go to prison. But I didn't even have $5, so they assigned me a court-appointed lawyer. I told him exactly what happened.

The attorney told me that they wanted me to sign a plea bargain. I said, "OK, but what does it say?" The plea bargain would state that I plead guilty to all charges, which meant 25 years in prison. That scared the shit out of me! 25 years in prison? No way. I felt as if I was going to pass out. I was dying inside.

The attorney assured me that 21 years would be suspended, and I would only have to do four in prison. But

I barely made it through five days in jail. How could I do prison time? I'm not a bad person. I didn't mean to hurt anybody. I was trying to take care of my children and make sure they were fed and make sure the rent was paid. But I know I was still wrong.

I said I wanted to go to trial. He told me that if I opted for trial the jury may sentence me to the whole 25 years. I said, "give me the paper, I'll sign it!"

As I contemplated going to prison, I knew I had to find someone to keep my kids while I was gone, but I did not have anybody. I had no one that would take care of them, love them, and protect them. My entire family was plagued with alcohol, drug, mental, and physical abuse. So much dysfunction there. I had no one to trust, no one to turn to. The only so-called normal people that I did know I met during the brief visit of James' family in eastern Kentucky.

I was terrified to go to prison. I knew I would not see my children, and I could not protect them. I know that I did the wrong thing and broke the law. There is no excuse for breaking the law and I take full responsibility. If I had it all to do over again, I would do it because I was trying to make sure that my children had the food that they needed and shoes on their feet. I did not think I had another way to get these things for them.

I only had 3 months with Shy before it was time for me to leave.

9

Dying on the Inside

In January of 1992, the time came to say goodbye to my children. I took Shy, Brittany, and Francheska to Paintsville, Kentucky to live with my mother-in-law. I barely knew James's parents, but they were the only people I knew that I felt would take good care of my children. Sadly, I didn't have anyone in my family that could. James's parents were very loving country people who were all about Sunday dinners and family functions. I was crushed, but thankful they agreed to take them.

To say it was hard to say goodbye to my girls would be an understatement. I would rather die than have suffered the heartbreak and heartache I felt that day. I worried that my kids wouldn't even remember me. I worried that I wouldn't be able to see them. I worried that prison was going to change me. I worried that someone would hurt me. I worried that prison would change me—and not for the better. I had no idea what would happen. Obviously, I had never done this before and was terrified.

I said goodbye and waited for my Greyhound bus. The 8-hour drive was the longest trip of my life. I just sat and thought about what my future was going to hold. My mind raced about my children and how much I was going to miss them. That was the worst part of it all. Being a mother was the greatest accomplishment of my life, and my children were the only people who ever loved me. They were my security, and I was theirs.

When I arrived at Tell City the next morning, I was ushered into court for my sentencing. I knew I would have to go to prison, but I was praying a miracle would happen and I didn't have to go. The next morning, I was nervous and scared.

After all that, my lawyer informed me that the court sentencing was postponed. "What do they mean it's postponed? I just said goodbye to my children! I can't go through that pain again," I told him. But he didn't care. As it turned out, the court postponed the sentencing for two-and-a-half weeks. So, I scrambled to find somewhere to stay until my court date came up again. My lawyer was the worst.

When I was escorted to the stand, they asked me if all this was true. Did I agree to all of this and that, and do I have anything to say? I said, "yes, I agree with what was stated." I also said that I had something that I wanted to say.

"The paper that I just signed to go to prison wasn't as hard as the paper I signed to have someone take custody of my children; someone I barely know. I'd go through all the abuse I ever had 1000 times if I knew in my heart my children would be ok," I whimpered through my tears.

After court was over, the jailer took me and told me to turn around. He then handcuffed my hands behind my back. I was in court alone! Why did they need to do that? I wasn't going to hurt anyone.

Then they transported me to the women's prison in Indiana. Other girls from various places in Indiana took the long ride with me to prison. When we arrived, they told us all to line up. We were told to follow the rules, wait our turn, and obey other directions. I listened because that's what I'm supposed to do; I am a follower. I always thought I was a leader, but at that time it didn't matter—I would be a good little follower.

The guard told me to take off all my clothes and get in the shower and then she looked through every part of my body for drugs. I remember the bitterly cold water and having to wash with lice shampoo. After that, I had to sit and cough, just in case there were drugs up my private parts. That was all new to me. I knew I didn't do drugs, but the guards didn't. I guess some people stash things up there, but I'm just not one of those people.

Since the prison didn't have a spot for me for the first 14 days, I was placed on the death row part of the prison! *Me. Sitting on death row. Me. I'm a giver. I'm a doer. I have a really big heart and follow most of the rules.* But, yes, I did break the law and now I had to follow all the rules. A price needed to be paid for what I did wrong.

The prison guards put me in this little cell with bright lights that stayed on 24 hours a day. I would look outside and listen to all the women there with their special languages on death row. Some women had recliners. Some women had a TV. I had nothing. Days went by. I was on the floor with women on death row and I didn't know what to do. I've never been around anybody that killed anybody.

I had the option to either go out for 15 minutes a day for recreation or you could make a phone call once a day.

When the guards would come in and ask me if I wanted to go to recreation. I said, "No, thank you." The guards asked me if I wanted to make a phone call, but I had nobody to call. Well, I had people to call but nobody that would accept my collect call. My family couldn't afford to accept my calls.

I was given a pencil about an inch-and-a-half long and 3 sheets of paper. I guess the short pencil was so an inmate wouldn't stab herself. I started to write with that pencil and paper about my experience being there so far. I wrote about how I got there and how I was feeling. But, if I had all the paper in the world, I wouldn't have been able to put my feelings down.

My clothes felt as thin as paper, too. I would freeze all day long.

All I could do was wait...and pray. I prayed that everything would be OK. Those 14 days came and went. As horrible as it was, I made it through those two weeks. How many days did I have left? 600 and something. Every day I counted down. Eventually, I'd forget a week or a month because I was so involved in working outside the prison that I just forgot.

After I got off death row, they put me into a classification area until they found out where I would be permanently incarcerated. Finally, they placed me in a small cell with one other woman from Fort Wayne who was in for drugs and prostitution. Mostly everybody I met was in there for drugs and prostitution. I met a couple of people who killed their children, their husbands, or somebody else. I even met a lady that killed her Sunday School teacher by beating her to death. I couldn't believe I was there. I wondered if God was punishing me.

My assignment was in the kitchen helping to cook, clean, get all the food ready, and dispense the leftover food. I had to make sure everyone's diet was right. It was OK food, but nothing to write home about. Even if I wanted to write home about the food, I didn't even have a stamp. I had no money. I couldn't buy any chips, pop or things like that. I lost a bunch of weight.

I was surrounded by a lot of different women and different personalities that I'd never experienced before. One night, I was sweeping the kitchen floor and getting ready to quit for the evening and go back to my bunk when this girl yelled at me for accidentally brushing the broom over her feet. She went off on me. She told me it was a bad luck thing and it meant she would go to jail. This was weird since we were already in prison. I told her I was sorry. The girl's name was Joy. But she certainly wasn't full of joy that day. Joy kind of scared me. I apologized because what else could I do? I knew I couldn't start shit up in there when I was the new girl.

I stayed there at the Indiana Department of Corrections for Women for about three months.

After that time, I was sent to a new place in Terra Haute at the Indiana Department of Correction. The new place had been a place for girls and boys but they just made it for women only a month before I got there. I went there and I was in dorm D. It was OK. There were about 12 people on each side of the dorm.

The summers in Terra Haute are very hot and the winters very cold. When I got there, they gave me my state clothes and my state work boots because my job would be helping clean up the parks and doing things like that. For being in prison, it was a high-paying job. I made $1.20 a day. We were paid every month, and I survived off the money I made while working. At the end of the month, my wages totaled about $27.00. It bought me a few snacks and some stamps.

I watched as everybody talked on the phone and had visitors. I missed talking to people and hearing my children's voices. I would have a chance once a month to call and talk to my children. Over time, I called a little bit less and less. They didn't want me to call collect. I would try to call my other family members, but they wouldn't take a collect call. So, I would just get on the phone and talk to an operator. I would shoot the shit with the operator for 15 minutes here and there. What else could I do? I had to think of something. I would also cut hair and draw for other women while there.

All in all, I made the best of the situation. I had a good reputation and was nobody's little bitch. I treated others with respect and acted nice till I didn't have to. There were a few times I needed to stand up for myself. In prison I had to be tolerant; I couldn't speak my mind to a certain extent. The guards and other women prisoners were always watching us.

One Fine Day

I enjoyed working on the road crew in the summer. I would get some sun and get to see people out in the real world. Even though we couldn't talk to the people in public, it was nice just to see them. We weren't allowed because of their safety and our safety. You just never knew what was going to happen. One day while I was working at this park called Turkey Run State Park cleaning up trash in front of the entrance of the hotel, this kind, older couple came to me and said, "Ma'am, can I talk to you for a second?"

"Who me?" I was like "no, I'm sorry I'm not allowed to talk to anybody." I had a vest on that had the initials of the prison I was incarcerated at. They didn't know that at the time. They were from out of town, and they didn't see the back of my vest. I tried walking away slowly and respectfully while they kept talking to me. I was worried about getting in trouble. They said it would only take a second.

Only a second? A second could get you in big-time trouble in prison. For some reason, I felt obligated to listen to what they had to say. She said "Ma'am, God sent me over to you. He told me to tell you to have faith. Have faith in Him. And whatever you're going through is going to pass, and you're going to make it through it."

What? GOD SENT THEM TO ME?? I didn't know what to say. How did these people know what's in my heart and what's in my mind? I was just picking up trash and God tells him to come over and tell me this. I remember thinking, *what's going on?* This made me feel awesome. I started to feel a little bit better about things on my mind—as though I could get through this stronger than before.

My prison guards came by to see what was going on, and I told them I was just leaving. As I walked away from this nice couple I said, "thank you." About a month or two later, I got a card in the mail. The card said, "praying for you and thinking of you." The kind man and woman I met briefly while I was working picking up trash sent me a letter and a $50 check! They told me they drove 4 hours to come and visit me, but because they were not on my visiting list, they couldn't get in. I could not believe that strangers would do something like this for me. They said it was because God told them, and God knew my pain. Wow, God felt my pain.

This older couple could have no idea to what extent their seemingly random act of kindness changed my life.

A couple of days later, I remember lying in bed and praying to God. I said "Lord, I'm going to ask you to do something and it's the hardest thing I ever had to do. God, I want to give you my children. I want to give you my children and put them in your arms and have your band of Guardian Angels around them each day of their life to guide and protect them each second while I'm away from them. God, I can't see you. God, I can't hear you. But, God, I feel you. I knew somehow You heard and felt me.

That day after my prayer, I felt the biggest relief and heaviness off my body just leave. *I can do this. I can do this*, I thought for the very first time. I gave my children to God knowing that He could care for them much better than I ever could. My time in prison became less stressful for the remaining time I had left. I was stronger than I had ever been in my life.

A couple of my friends visited me while in prison. My friend Tina came with my grandma. Once a year, we were able to have a big meal brought to us. My grandmother brought me a McDonald's cheeseburger. Even though it was cold and stale, I hadn't had Mcdonald's in a month and I was grateful for that burger.

A few months later, my friend Charlie came. He was a truck driver like my brother. He brought with him every kind of food a person could possibly think of: Kentucky fried chicken, Taco Bell, Pizza Hut, candy, pop—everything just for me. But, the guards wouldn't let me have it! The cheeseburger my grandma bought counted as my one meal per year. That's just my luck. Even though I couldn't have the food that Charlie brought, I was just glad to see him. The downside was that after each visit, we'd have to be strip-searched. It was humiliating but it was the rule.

My husband James came one time to see me. He had just been released from a prison stay a few months earlier, so he took the kids from his parents. He brought my children with him for a visit. It was an awesome day! But it was also a sad day. It was great to see them smile and laugh, hold them and listen to them talk. I got to see my babies. I loved it.

Ches didn't say much during the visit. She was eight years old by that time, Brittany was three, and Shy was an infant. Ches had always been on the quiet side, but she looked terrified. I thought seeing me in prison just made her nervous. (Little did I know at the time why she was so scared.) We all sat around outside at the picnic table. I enjoyed our short visit. The kids had to get back soon.

Inmates were not allowed to bring anything given to us back inside the prison, or we would be in big trouble. Brittany had picked me a flower—a little piece of a weed off the ground. I wasn't going to give that up. So, I tucked it away to keep it with me and still have that little piece of weed to this day preserved in a photo album. Some things I just couldn't give up. That memory was priceless because it just wasn't only that weed that was important. It was from a little girl that I miss so much who picked it for me.

I managed to make the best of it of the remaining time I had left. Knowing that I had finished one year made me feel like the last year would be easier. It felt as if I was on a downhill slide from there. In the State of Indiana, you only need to serve half of your time. That meant that instead of four years, I had two years to serve.

When it was almost time to be released, they sent me to a work in a step-down program. They call it a pre-release. It was horrible. Again, I had to stay in a room with just two people, I could not go outside. I could not do anything. All the things that I enjoyed while I was working outside of the prison were stripped away. Even though it was still prison, I got used to a certain quality of life. It got stripped away. The only upside was that I had the chance to call home several times to talk to my children.

I received a letter from Ches and Brittany's school expressing their concerns about my children. The school administrator told me something that I never would have imagined would happen to my children—he said they thought that my girls were being molested. I remember saying, "what do you mean molested? What's going on?"

So, I called James and I said, "what are they talking about?" He said the school thinks that he's molesting the children and they might be taken away from him. Of course, he told me that they were crazy for saying that, and I was crazy for believing them. But I knew it was true.

As terrible as prison was, my worst nightmare still awaited me.

10

Holler Hell

The end of my prison time finally came. I was so happy to be going home to my children. I would have thought that—after two years—my husband, mom, or somebody like that would be picking me up from prison and be happy to do it. But, no, that wasn't the case. I had no ride. The city where my children were living was about six hours away from the Terre Haute prison. Apparently, my husband James did not have a decent left car to drive. Being a mechanic, I would have thought he'd have reliable transportation. Although disappointed, I wasn't surprised.

Fortunately, I found a ride. I met a man named Joe when I worked on the road crew in prison—he was my boss. He was a very nice, older man and would bring me cigarettes, food, pizza, white castles, and all kinds of goodies that I couldn't get from the inside. Joe knew my situation. I didn't use him, nor did I lie to him about anything going on in my life. He was just a very good friend. Joe offered to pick me up from prison, as well as another friend of mine I met while there, Darlene.

Darlene served prison time for drinking and driving. She had killed a young man who was getting ready to graduate high school. She was working in California at a bank. She was like a vice president or something like that. She came to Indianapolis for a Christmas party, and after the party, she drove to her hotel and that's when the accident happened. Besides having to be sent to prison the judge had her watch a video of the young man's class graduation with his name on a chair. His family had taken the video. It was too much for her. She couldn't take the guilt. She was a very sweet, polite, smart lady.

When I first met Darlene, she was a plus-sized gal. By the time she was released, she got down to 100 pounds. She looked horrible. She was so depressed and so distraught about how she killed that young man. I hate that there were two lives taken: the young man she killed, and her life had been lost over with the guilt from it.

While being in prison together, Darlene and I were there for each other. About a month after I was released, she had her husband sent me a box with all my favorite snacks, perfumes, and soaps. It was nice to feel like a normal person for once. It was a long time since I got to have these things and use the stuff I received.

Joe and Darlene picked me up from the pre-release center in Indianapolis, IN on March 17, 2994. (Joe had picked up Darlene about a month earlier.) They dropped me off at my grandma Margaret's house in Tell City, Indiana. I stayed there overnight until James could pick me up the next day.

I was very nervous about being out. The next day James came by himself to pick me up. Immediately we headed to Paintsville, KY to see my three girls. I was so excited! I had only seen them one time while I was serving time in prison. Since I had to leave Shy when she was an infant, I hadn't had the opportunity to bond with her. I was hoping that she would remember me in some way, but I knew only time would tell.

On the long ride from Indiana to Kentucky, James and I talked about what went on while I was incarcerated. We talked about the good things and the bad things.

In hindsight, I honestly think everybody should be sent to prison at least one time in their life. We wouldn't take things for granted as we all do. All the activities that the average person is used to doing such as kissing your children goodnight, driving to the mall, visiting friends, and opening your fridge to find something to eat, would have renewed meaning. You just don't understand until your children are taken away from you how your life could change in one moment. But, in the end, all that was taken could be restored—but the choice is yours. We have the power to make our life better. We can't go back, but we can go forward and make better choices.

A few days after I settled in, I remember walking to the store with my children and putting my hand up on my chest to feel if I had my badge on me. While in prison, there were so many rules to follow and so many things to remember. I had to make sure I didn't forget my badge—ever. I was only in prison for two years, but it felt like forever. I was happy to be out, but I was still terrified. I knew the day I was released I did not want to be with James, but I didn't know where to go. The most important thing at that moment was to get custody of my kids back.

"Painsville"

The next few years would be the hardest thing I ever had to live through in my life. The only good thing that came after my release was becoming pregnant with my son. Dylan was born on Christmas Eve—December 24, 1994—less than ten months after my release.

When we picked up my children from the babysitter's home in Paintsville, we moved into James's trailer. Life in Paintsville, Kentucky was horrible. I HATED IT THERE. The locals had odd ways of doing things. As a woman, I was expected to clean, look after my husband and children, cook dinner, and then clean again afterward. The husband and children always ate first. Sometimes I didn't eat.

We moved many times while living in Paintsville because James didn't pay the rent. Sometimes we would get kicked out because James had so much junk in the yard or broken-down cars. Other times we were evicted because he didn't keep the lawn cut. I remember mowing the grass when I was 8-1/2 months pregnant with Dylan. Each time I saw a snake in the grass, my heart would beat so hard that it felt like a heart attack. There were so many snakes that I mowed over in that tall, overgrown lawn. The thought of a slimy snake that close to me made me feel so anxious and so scared while I was mowing but it had to be done so that we didn't get evicted again. I had to have a place for my children to live. I was always hot and sweaty during the summer in Kentucky while I pushed the mower back and forth in front of the trailer to cut the grass.

I tried to look at the positives in my life as a coping mechanism rather than looking at how hard things were. It was a matter of survival. At one point we lived in a little small two-bedroom trailer with a wood floor that barely covered the whole trailer. In some spots, I could see the dirt ground under the trailer. I tried to make the best of each house we lived in. James would never take the trash to the dump so it would pile up in the front yard of the trailer, attracting mice, rats, snakes, and maggots. I hated living like this. I knew I deserved better than this, but I couldn't see a way out.

One beautiful sunny day when the weather was just right, I wanted to clean and get stuff done. I determined to take care of that mess of trash. I went to the side of the trailer and got the gasoline can we used, or that I used, to mow the grass and I poured it all over the big trash pile. I knelt next to the trash pile to look for a good piece of paper to burn and start this fire. As I lit my little Bic© lighter, I didn't expect it to ignite and blow up with such force! Something in the pile was combustible and the explosion blew me back about ten feet. The hairs on my arms, eyebrows and a few on my head were burned off. Even though I thought I had blown myself up and was dying, I was very happy about getting rid of the trash pile.

There were many times while living in that forsaken town that I thought I was going to die. The kitchen was so small that we kept a fridge outside in front of the trailer because there wasn't room inside. We plugged it in using an extension cord. One day while it was raining, I ran across the yard and stepped on that bare extension cord! Once again, I thought I was dead. I couldn't move at all. I was freezing in place, just feeling the electric shock all through my body.

I often thought about ways I could escape James. One time, I had an idea. I told James I missed my family and I wanted to visit them. He said that's fine. He let me take Dylan and Brittany but insisted Shy and Ches stay with him. Of course, I didn't want any of them to stay with him. That monster I married was destroying my children.

So, I took Dylan and Brittany to go visit our family in Tell City. My mom, Angie, Margret, and other family members were there too. While in Tell City, I planned my escape so I could get all my kids to safety. I signed up for government housing and landed a 3-bedroom apartment In Hawesville, Kentucky.

I felt very confident that I would finally be able to break free of James. I planned to go back and get my kids and bring them to my HUD-provided housing—without him. It felt so liberating.

James would never be able to hurt them or me again, I thought. But I was wrong. James called me and asked when I was coming back. I told him that I missed my family so much that I got an apartment up here. He freaked out. He said, "you better get your fucking ass home if you know what's good for you." I told him it would all be OK and that it's just a place for us to stay when we come and visit, and that I'd be home soon.

In the middle of the night, James came after me. I was awaked by a loud knock on the door. It was James. He came in busting through, yelling, hollering, pushing me. He asked me what the hell I think I'm doing. I played stupid. I acted as if this was the best for both of us. It seemed like I was always playing a game with him since my release from prison so that I could get away from him. I always had to be on my toes.

He then took me to my bedroom and push me down on the bed. He held his gun in his hands, as he always did. But then he put that gun to my head and said, "Dorothy, I've told you time after time if you leave me, you are going to be the reason your babies will die."

I panicked and told him I wasn't leaving him. That I was just trying to make it easier for when we traveled. He didn't believe me, so he didn't leave. He stayed there for a while with Ches and Shy. I didn't know what to do next.

Some say that it's easy to leave an abusive relationship—but I assure you that it's not. That situation is complicated and scary. No one knows what it's like unless you have been there yourself.

My escape plan had failed for the moment. He moved into that apartment with us. He would leave for days or weeks at a time, and I didn't know when he would come back. He was always out doing drugs or cheating. I would wish and pray that he would get in a horrible car crash and die, or something like that. I know that's bad to say but I don't take it back. It's easy for someone to judge me for thinking or saying that but it's true and I don't regret saying it.

A house came up for sale. It was on a contract sale, so we got it. James had a little company to work on heavy equipment in coal mines. This meant he was gone a lot and that was OK with me. It would give me more time to be stronger and to think of a way to get away from him.

One day I told him that I couldn't take it anymore. He was mad and told me that I couldn't leave. There was a strength in me that just said "DO IT NOW" so I got a place to live next to the police station in Cannelton, Indiana, a town right next to Tell City. There was nothing much in this town except churches and bars, but I was so glad that the place I found to move to was next to the police station. God was on my side.

During this time, I would write letters and put them in different places or send them to family members or friends to let them know that if I died, it was James and to please take care of my kids. I wrote each of my children a letter telling them how much I loved them and how special they were to me. I would write what a gift from God they were to me. I told them how sorry I was for how their life had turned out. Every time I wrote a letter to them, I would cry. It broke my heart for them.

I grew accustomed to the pain of being hit by him. It was just something that always happened. I kept on playing the game in my mind thinking about what was going to be my next move. This mental game that I was trying to play with James to make him think everything was going to be OK until I could get us completely away from him. I just needed to live by myself and get away from him for a little bit. We would go back to visit his family off and on. His family was very nice, but they always took his side with things. And that's OK because family is supposed to have your back. They always knew he was having sex with other girls and doing drugs and drinking. His family never told me. I would always find out in a different way. I would always be the one making this up he would say.

James's brother Joey would always try to get with me. He would say I want a woman just like you that cleans and cooks and has babies. I never told James about this. James would have killed Joey. Even though I knew that James had a temper and was capable of terrible violence, I would flirt back with Joey. I thought in my mind this is a way I could get back at James. I wasn't proud of myself for this at all, but it was a release for a moment. I enjoyed someone being nice and paying attention to me. Somebody enjoyed me.

James finally got the hint that our relationship was ending. He became even more involved in drugs and drinking. He kept Ches and Shy with him. He had lost the house that we were buying together because he never paid the bills. He got a camper in the middle of nowhere in Hawesville. I never went there to visit. I guess he didn't want me to know where he lived. They would all stay in this little bitty camper while I stayed in my trailer next to the police station.

Again, James came after me. I felt as if I would never escape him. I had my own office in a house for a medical equipment business. While I was at work one day, James came in. I was the only one there because I always got to work early. (It's my OCD. I always have to be really early.) James came in there and took me by my wrists. He grabbed me so hard that my watch broke off my wrist and my chair broke. He said, "you may be living away from me, but you'll never escape me". Then James punched me and hit me again. He always did this.

One day, he had to go to work and was going to bring Ches and Shy for me to watch. I would have all of my kids with me and thought that this would be a time to get us away from him. He came back early from work to pick up the kids and he was high on something. This time it was the worst yet.

When James came to pick up the kids early, the look in his eyes was like looking into the eyes of the devil. He was standing at the foot of my bed with his gun pointed right at me. I had been asleep and woke up to see him there. He said take off your clothes. I said, "No. Let me just sleep. Please let me just sleep."

He was so high on something that I guessed was meth. He would shoot up with needles and I would find them all over the place. I did what he told me to. I took my clothes off. He still had the gun pointed at me. He told me to do different things that I didn't really want to do at all. No one would ever want to do these things. He told me to do sexual things to myself—sick stuff that only a man like him could want. He never let the gun go. He put me face down and laid on me. He pulled my hair so hard that my head was going up and down with each pull and punch. He had hands full of my hair. Later I saw that it was all over the place where he had pulled it out. I had hair in my mouth from him pulling it out. I would try to spit it out of my mouth the best I could while he had his hand over my mouth so tight. He was raping me in every way possible. I just cried and begged. I was trying to talk and beg him to please let me go. The more I yelled and cried, the worst it got. I kept moving around trying to get out of the body lock he had on me. He was too strong.

James almost killed me that time while he was raping me. At one point my head was hanging over the bed. Everything was upside down. I looked through the hall of the trailer. Dylan and Brittany were sound asleep on a recliner. Ches and shy were all cuddled up together on the couch sleeping. His hand was still tight over my mouth so hard. I couldn't breathe. I was gasping for air and slobber was all over my face and snot from my nose. I was a mess

I was dying. I knew this day was going to come. This day was for real. It wasn't a shock from an electrical cord or fire from where I stupidly piled gasoline on the trash. I was dying. I could feel my eyes rolling in the back of my head. There was more slobber from my mouth all over his hand and all over my face from trying to wiggle and squirm and get away from him.

I looked at Dylan. He was two years old. All I could think of while I was trying to get my next breath was that Dylan would never know how much his mother loved him. He wouldn't remember me when he grew up to be a man. He wouldn't remember me because he was too young.

James finally let go of my mouth and I gasped for air. I started breathing heavily at first and I was in shock. My mind was still processing how James had raped and beat me while a gun was pointed at my head. No one should ever have to go through this, but it was just another day in my life.

James was so high, so he just left to go find some more drugs. I called my friend Jick as soon as he left. She came right to my house even though she lived out in the country about 25 minutes away. It seemed like it was forever before she got there. It was a Sunday night. She told me that we should go to the police. I said, "I can't. You don't understand he would kill me." I knew he would.

I thought that I couldn't go to the police, but I did. They were right next door. I walked in and told the officer what happened. I told him that I need help and I had just been raped. He had told me there was nothing they could do until Monday morning.

I said, "you don't understand. I don't have till Monday morning. He will be back any moment and will kill my children and me. I need help!" I wanted to puke; I was so scared.

As we were walking out of the police station, I saw a victim's advocate card. I called the number on the card. I told them what was going on. Thankfully, they got things moving fast—a nice lady got a room for us at a local motel. We all were so scared. I couldn't think straight.

I had a sense that time had run out for my kids and me. While we were in the hotel room, I changed the color of my hair thinking somehow this would help me not to be recognized by him. I know it was stupid. My kids and I lay in bed and watched TV. There was a metal door keeping anyone from entering. It did make me feel safe, but we couldn't live there forever. We couldn't leave or go anywhere or talk to anybody, because nobody could know where we were, especially James.

Ches told me while sitting on the bed at the hotel that James had been raping them for years. She went into depth about what he did. Great depth. It was so difficult to hear what Ches was telling me about what he had been doing to her and Brittany. When I had gotten released from prison, it wasn't like I could just walk away from James. It wasn't because he was my husband. I had to pretend like I didn't know or believe her. I DID BELIEVE HER.

After two days I couldn't stand being in the hotel room any longer. I had to get out for a moment. The kids and I thought we could sneak over to my sister, Angie's house. She lived in a little trailer along the flood wall in Cannelton.

Ches begged to go to church with Angie that night. I said OK at first but then I changed my mind and wanted her to just come back with me. Ches was upset, which wasn't new. She was often upset with me, and she would be many more times in the future. I didn't parent her the way I would have because of the guilt I felt from her being abused. A mother always wants to protect her child. It was my job, and I couldn't. I couldn't protect any of us, including myself.

I knew James would figure that I'd go to Angie's, so my kids and I went back to the hotel. My best friend Tina called me later that day in a panic. Her mom had a police scanner. Everybody had a scanner in Cannelton, that's just the way it was. We all wanted to know what was going on in the small town.

Tina told me that there was something that came over the scanner about Angie's trailer. I thought that after church she may have had too many beers and got arrested for something. Angie often did that kind of thing. But this time—that wasn't it. James had broken into her trailer while she was at church with her husband. My nephew, George, was waiting for someone to get home to unlock the door. He was 14 at the time and had two of his friends with him. George walked into the trailer and James was in there.

George had no idea what was going on. Poor guy. When Angie and her husband Ronnie got home from church,

Ronnie walked toward the trailer first. As he approached the porch, he could see that James was pointing a gun at George and his friends. Angie's husband ran back to her and told her what was going on. Angie ran up in the trailer and started going off on James. She didn't think of the fact that he had a gun. As a mother, she only knew that her son was there with his friends.

James held the gun to Angie's head and told her to shut up and sit down. By this time the police were called by a neighbor. James kept asking Angie where we were. Where were his kids? She told him she didn't know, but of course, she was lying to protect us. He kept demanding she tell him. The swat team, helicopters, and the police in all the surrounding towns showed up. Several detectives and even the local news people were there.

Hours went by. I was on the phone with Tina listening to all this happening. James was kneeling in the living room sporting several of his guns. He had a belt around his neck full of bullets. We all understood that James was crazy, but this was beyond anything we had imagined.

I knew James would kill each one of them if they didn't tell him where we were.

11

Aftermath

The intensity grew with every minute. James called his mom telling her how much he loved her because he knew this was the last day he was going to be alive; he was either going to find me and kill me and then kill himself, or the police were going to kill him.

Hours went by. Helicopters flew back and forth, and news reporters were all over the place. It was crazy!

As I listened to the report on the radio, I couldn't bear the thought of somebody dying because of my choices. I had to do something. So, I got in my car and drove to Angie's trailer. I saw the detective who was the head of the operation, Jerry Belcher. Ironically, he was also the man that arrested me a few years back! I walked up to him. There were so many lights from all the different police cars and the helicopter swarming the trailer, and the sun had gone down by this point, so those lights lit up the whole scene.

Detective Belcher was on a phone trying to talk to James. James told him that just like the murder of the wife and kids in Jasper a few weeks back, there was going to be the same thing here. I didn't remember that event exactly, but I knew that what happened in Jasper was a bloodbath.

I asked Detective Belcher to let me talk to him. *Please* let me talk to him, I begged. The SWAT team surrounded the trailer and were looking in every window They were watching his every move. They also watched every move that Angie and the three boys made, too.

Again, I begged the detective to please let me talk to James. He told me to get out of there—to leave immediately. The SWAT team had messaged the detective that James knew I was outside and that he had his gun pointing at me.

So, I left. I didn't want to, but they made me. I went back to the motel to listen until everything was over. It seemed like it took a lifetime for it to end.

Before the hostage situation, when I had gone to the police and told them about what happened, I begged them at that time to do something because I was very afraid that something like this would happen. I filed a report about how James had violently raped me and how he had repeatedly molested Ches and Brittany. Because I wanted to make sure that James would go to prison for life for what he had done to my children, the detective told me I would need to provide some DNA. He said that they would need some unwashed panties.

A police officer then took me to my trailer to try to locate some evidence. The detective needed some additional things from my house for DNA. He said he needed the last pair of panties Ches had on before we left to go into hiding.

I found a pair of panties and he put them in a bag for evidence. While we were walking back to his police car, James drove by. I said, "there he is, there he is!" I was so scared I hid underneath the police car. The police officer called for backup, but James didn't stay too long. He immediately took off.

I know the police tried to resolve the issue at the time, but nothing happened. An officer went to James's camper in Kentucky, but he lied to them about who he was. James said no, his name is not James May. He told them his name was Joey May. He and his brother looked alike, so maybe the police thought he was telling the truth.

James asked, "What is this about?" The police officer told James he needed to ask him some questions regarding his wife and children. James knew very well what it was about. He knew I had gone to the police and told them everything that had happened. But he determined not to go to prison again, and he sure wasn't going to go to prison for molesting children. In prison, child molesters don't do well. No matter how strong of a man you are or how strong your mind is, you *will* get hurt.

When James realized that I had filed a report with the police about how he raped me and repeatedly molested my children while I was in prison, that's when he went to my sister's house to kill me. When I wasn't there, he held my family hostage at gunpoint.

As I sat there helplessly listening to the police monitor, I called James. I begged him not to hurt Angie and the boys. "I will come back," I lied to him. "Everything will be the same as he would want it to be." But James wouldn't listen.

James kept telling me that they all going to die. Again and again, he said that they were all going to die. He even gave a time limit on when he would kill them. I hung up and started freaking out. There was nothing I could do except sit there and listen to hear what was happening.

Around this time my sister Angie asked James if she could go to the restroom. The three young teenagers were sitting on the couch and as Angie walked by them, she whispered to them, "I have a plan." I don't know exactly what she said but something like that. When she went to the bathroom, she put her hands together and prayed while she sat on the toilet. The SWAT team looked in the window, but she didn't see them.

Angie prayed, "Lord, please let this end. Please give me the strength to overpower him and save these children in there on the couch." As she walked back into the living room, she motioned to the boys that she was going to get the gun. She spoke quietly and so fast I'm surprised that they all understood the plan.

James knelt on the ground, smoking a cigarette in one hand, and held a gun with the other hand in between his thighs. He squeezed it between his legs so that no one could grab it. Angie walked over to him and, in one swift motion, pushed him over as hard as she could. The gun fell to the ground from between his legs. The boys jumped on him, tackled him, and held him while Angie took the gun.

Angie held the gun out the window screaming. I got the gun! I got the gun! Help me, help! As the cops rushed in, the boys got up off James and the police took over. About eight police officers were coming all at once at James. They all were wrestling around trying to tackle James down. He was very strong, and it took them a minute to do it but they got him. Finally, they got him. He was in that police car, and everybody was safe.

The SWAT team was very pleased that no one was injured during the standoff, obviously, but I wasn't. I wish I could have gotten that lucky and the police killed him, but it didn't happen. I knew that would be the only way my children and I would ever finally be released from the grip of this monster. Even though I did feel some relief with James being arrested, the pain that he caused didn't go away.

In fact, the pain would continue to grow. The next day the welfare system inserted itself because the children had been molested. There was so much going on that I just didn't know what to do. The worst part was that I knew I would need to face him again at his trial.

I told the police officers and the child welfare people everything that I knew. And even though I wasn't the perpetrator, I felt I was the bad one; I was the one who "allowed" all this to happen. It was a lot to carry.

Finally, James was locked up in jail. He was charged by the State of Indiana with five counts of kidnapping, possessing a gun as a felon, and a couple of other things for the hostage situation. But, since James' trailer was located just across the border in Kentucky, their district attorney took over those charges. The grand jury indicted him in KY for the molestation charges. A lady detective was working with me for many months on it, but they had to wait for his trial in Indiana to be done with their charges. That seemed to take forever.

James refused to go to court. He hung from the bars like a monkey as if he was crazy. He is crazy. The judge held some of his hearings in his cell because James refused to go anywhere. Nobody could confine him, and sadly, they were playing his game. They were now under his control, too.

As hard as it may be to believe, the drama wasn't over. James finally "agreed" to appear for a hearing. During the ride to the courthouse in the police cruiser, he was in the front seat (somehow) making friends with the officer that was driving him there. His name was Lenny.

On the way to court James, while handcuffed and shackled, somehow managed to get the gun away from the officer driving. Lenny jumped out of the car and tried wrestling James to the ground and recover his weapon. At that moment, a Branchville prison guard drove by. There was a prison down the road, so I guess the employees were getting off work. The guard witnessed the police car and the struggles Lenny was having trying to save his own life from that monster. The guard quickly got out and got the gun away from James.

Tons of officers flocked to where this was going on. James went back to jail and received even more charges of attempted murder on a police officer and attempted escape. The newspaper said that James wanted to be shot and killed. That was his plan. It never happened, but I wished it would have.

After many months of court days, James was finally sentenced to 84 years in prison.

He's still in prison today. Our lives are safe now from the monster that hurt us many times. But my struggle didn't end there.

12

Blood and Tears

After they locked up James, I would take the two children we had together, Shy and Dylan, to visit him in prison. Even though I felt obligated to let them see their father, I was scared to death every time I saw him. Literally. He told me multiple times that he would kill me when he got out, and I still believe to this day that this will be how I will die. One day, when James is an old man out of prison, there will be a knock on my door or be sleeping in my bed. He will kill me.

When Shy and Dylan visited with their dad, they were scared to talk. Even though Shy was his baby girl, she feared him. As terrified as I was, I resolved to let them develop their own opinion of him. It wasn't for me, even as their mother, to tell them who to love or not love. If I took that option away from them, I felt certain they would hate me someday. They would hate me because I didn't give them a chance to know their father.

As the kids got older, they would write him in prison. James would always write back and preach to them about how to live right. He had no idea of how to do that himself, of course. As time moved on, the visits were less and less. Because of my fear, I stopped going after a few visits and family members would take them.

From the beginning, I promised to be honest with my children. I told them what their father had done. As Dylan and Shy grew up, they discovered more and more about their dad, and they did not want to see him anymore. When the dust settled, both of them had a hard time getting over what their father did to Chess and Brittany, their older half-sisters. They felt guilty for what he did, but they still loved him. After all, James was their father.

Continually, I reassured them that they had no reason to feel guilty. I told Shy and Dylan that it was OK to love him still. Their choice is their own of how they felt about them Him. I can't take that choice from them. A lot of my friends looked down on me because they couldn't understand why I encouraged them to have a relationship with their father in prison. They wanted a dad. Don't we all?

Growing up, I always told my children they are just like the company they keep. If they hang out with people doing bad stuff, they will also be in trouble for it too, even if they did nothing wrong. Dylan sometimes would say, "Mom. I can't help from being bad and hanging with the wrong crowd. I'm going to be just like my dad. I just know it."

I would assure Dylan that he didn't really know his father. He only knew him from his short few visits. "You can't be like him if you don't know him," I told him. "Be like you, son. Grow to be a good father—that's the most important thing you can do."

Sister, Sister

Around this time, Angie met the love of her life, Jeff, through a friend. He was in prison for a long time, at least 10 years, because he robbed a pharmacy. He was a good-looking guy, very well-built, and a very nice man. Prison doesn't define a person. It only makes the person that is weak become something they are not.

When Jeff got out of jail, Angie was in. She was arrested for taking drugs into another prison for one of her friends. Before her husband Jeff was released, I had custody of her two children Brandi and George. I loved them as if they were mine. I still think of them as my own and love them so very much. They had a hard life and saw and experienced so many tough and tragic things while growing up, just as I did.

We welcomed Jeff into our family. I drove Grandma Margret to Indianapolis to pick Jeff up from prison. We waited outside for him. It was our first time meeting him and we welcomed him into our family. We had talked to him plenty of times on the phone. He was the same in person as he was on the phone. We stopped to get gas and he got out to pump it for us because he was a gentleman. He was an all-around good, loving man.

As he started pumping the gas for grandma's car, he didn't know how to use the gas pump. It was digital. They didn't have that when he went into prison. I said, "Hey, let me help you." I said, "Things change every day out here in the world. You never know what's going to be new one day to the next day." I didn't want him to feel embarrassed, so I tried to make fun of it. I never like hurting anybody's feelings or telling anybody how I felt about them. I guess maybe I was scared. Or maybe I just didn't like hurting anybody's feelings.

On the ride home, we talked a lot and got to know each other more. When he got home, my grandpa put him to work helping clean up the chicken coop and some other work around their house. They let him stay there awhile and the kids loved him. Angie's kids adored him. They called him "dad." He was a good father figure for them even though they didn't know him very well. He showed them love. Good, solid love. The unconditional love that every child needs and craves for life.

After a year Angie was released from prison. She had lost a bunch of weight and looked again like a model. She seemed just like a beautiful teenager, and I was so proud of her. She seemed like she was doing well in life. Grandma, of course, bought them a house and set it up for them. She bought Angie a car and everything else again for her.

During the next year, Angie and Jeff grew together as a family. Angie was as happy as she had ever been in life. But Jeff only lived in that happiness for a short time. One day, a year later, they went swimming with a few friends at German ridge park. There was a beautiful lake there. They went to hang out and skinny dip, or whatever, to have a good time. It was innocent fun with a bunch of friends and family. I found out later that they were drinking and doing some pills there, too.

On that day, I was at my grandma Margaret's cleaning. While I was there, Margaret received a call from a forest ranger. He asked if this was Margret. She said, "Yes, it is. How can I help you?"

The ranger told her that we needed to immediately go to the hospital. My grandmother was freaking out. She was praying and talking in tongues, which I never really understood. Grandma would pray many times at church and hold her hands up and talk in a language I never understood. She would pray for God to come and take her while I was under the bench. I would have a pen and paper and a mint that she had given me so I wouldn't be noisy and fidgety. I would sit and draw and listen to everybody preach and sing and fall and get prayed for. At that moment, she prayed louder and more fervently than ever.

I drove Grandma Margret to the hospital. On the way there we received a phone call on grandma's flip cell phone. It was Angie. She said, "Jeff's dead! Jeff's dead!" We could hardly understand what was going on. We just drove to the hospital and walked into the emergency room area. There was Angie in the hallway laying on Jeff's body trying to breathe in his mouth to get him to have one more breath. They were out swimming in the lake and Jeff was out near the ropes swimming around, having a good time, and enjoying the sun. Angie was at the bank when she looked around and she asked where Jeff was. Everybody began looking. They saw him struggling in the water towards the ropes. One of their friends Rick, we all know him as Eight Ball, tried to swim for him but they couldn't find him. Someone called the police, and the forest ranger came and called for an ambulance. They pulled his body from the lake, but he was already gone.

Angie never got over Jeff's death. She loved him and missed him so much. I don't think any man ever loved her as much as Jeff did. And she never loved anybody again to the same extent as Jeff. Grandpa Henry was very sad about what happened to Jeff, too. Grandpa Henry was one to never share his money with anyone, but he bought Jeff's gravestone. It was as beautiful as a gravestone could be with Jeff's name carved in it and said, "I am a loving father, husband, and son."

Angie's name was engraved on the other side of the tombstone Grandpa Henry purchased, as well. I will admit, it seemed strange seeing my sister's name there. She was alive. . . at least a part of her was alive. A big part of her was gone when Jeff died. Angie never got over the hurt from Jeff dying. I know a lot of it was the love that she lost, but I think some of it was guilt.

Angie didn't do well alone. Not long after, maybe a year, she got married to a man named Ronnie. He was a little weird, but everyone liked him. They felt sorry for him because Angie wore the pants in that family. She was the boss. She could do and come and go, whatever she wanted. As I said before, when she was good, she was good. When she was bad, she was bad. Her old ways came back out.

Angie and mom kept their bond together and always lived together wherever Angie lived. Mom would either live with Angie or she would find an apartment right next to her. They both kept a very clean house. Angie's house was always real homey, always real inviting. It would be the house where you'd want to go lay on the couch watch TV, eat a good meal, and fall asleep. Mom's house never had much just the basics. They both always had incense burning. I'm sure it was because of all the pot smoke.

I called Angie one day because I was finally fed up with how she was treating me. She was very mean to me. I allowed her to keep the babysitting money that the government gave me to watch my children for many months. I finally got the balls to call her. Honestly, I was too scared to do it in person. I called her and I said, "Hey, I'm really upset." and I just went off on her. We were both yelling and saying things to each other that we didn't mean. I went to bed that evening still mad. The next morning while sitting on the couch getting ready for work the phone rang. It was my mom. She told me in a voice that I never heard before and I could barely understand, yet, I understood the word clearly and it's weird to explain. The words that I heard on the phone were "Dottie, Angie is dead!"

I said, "What do you mean, she is dead? What, no, this is not true." I ran out of the house trying to find a ride to her. I didn't want to believe it. I thought it wasn't true.

But then, again, I'm surprised it hadn't happened already with the decisions and the number of drugs that they both had taken together. Still, I never wanted it to happen. Angie was 39 she just got her teeth all pulled and was excited about getting her false teeth. She was in a lot of pain at night and she had got some pain pills. She had some friends that lived upstairs in the apartment above her. It was the party place. The whole house had drugs, such as meth, and alcohol.

Angie was found at the foot of her bed downstairs lying face down with her hands underneath her face as if she were praying when she passed. I can't say really what happened to Angie and how she died I could only conclude that too many pain pills or drugs were taken or too many shot up that night. Her husband at that time, Ronnie, was there. He went to bed knowing that my sister was lying on the floor. Did he know she was dead? We don't know. We will never know. Did he care? Probably not. I hate to say that, but he was just that kind of guy. Heartless. He would work and Angie would still rule the house as she did with the other men in her life in the past.

My heart was breaking. I loved my sister so much. What hurt most was my mom lost her oldest child, her best friend, her everything. Angie always took care of mom the best she could. Mom was worried about who was going to care for her now. I promised her that I would take care of her.

Not even a couple of months after Angie died Ronnie remarried. As I said, he was just weird that way. I could never understand him and the things he did. I didn't think much of him or hung around with him. I only did it because my sister was married to him.

Angie already had her gravestone. The only thing she didn't have on it was the date that she died. I would be the one to take care of it and make sure they would put it on there. I'm sure grandma would've if she was alive as grandma did everything for her. (Grandma Margaret passed away a few years before Angie from a stroke.) I called the people who did this kind of thing and told them the day that Angie died. Even though I double and triple-checked it, I got the date wrong. It's good that Angie had a good sense of humor because I gave her three extra days to be alive. I wish I could've given her forever to be alive. I wish I could have given her enough time to see her children and grandchildren grow up to be parents and grandparents.

Mom was heartbroken when Angie died. Angie was not only her daughter but her best friend. She said to me, "Who will take care of me now?" I promised her that I would always take care of her.

At Angie's funeral, I walked past the coffin where her swelled body lay. I went over to Mom, got down on my knees, and took her hands in mine. I looked into her sad eyes and told her that I will always be there for her.

Mom tried to do life on her own for a few years, but things just didn't work out well for her. Between the drugs and her health issues, she couldn't manage to be alone. because of the drugs and health issues. So, to keep my promise, I found a house big enough for me, my children, and my mom. I fixed it up for her and made sure she had everything she needed.

I wanted to give my mom everything she never had—or everything that I never had. I wanted to spoil her like I wanted to be spoiled when I was young. Actually, I never wanted to be spoiled; I just wanted my mom's attention and affirmation. I wanted to have my needs met. I gave all that to my mom, because I loved her very much. It's a different type of love I held for my mom. I would take her medicine and dispense it to her as needed. I told her that she needed to stop doing drugs. She wasn't allowed to get into any more trouble. I told her to relax and enjoy life. Mom would get mad when I talked to her about her past. She always tried to hide it from me. I guess she forgot that I lived through a lot of it with her. She forgot that I was exposed to it while she was supposed to be taking care of me. I learned a lot about drugs and stuff while growing up with mom and Angie.

Mom needed a lot of care, and it made me feel good to be needed. I felt sorry for her and for all the pain she endured from being abused. Men beat her. Drugs overcame her. Even so, she was my mom no matter what. She developed hepatitis from using dirty needles and knee replacement surgeries from taking a few falls. She contracted cancer when she was seventy years old. She said, "Dottie, I'm going to die." I assured her that after what she had already survived, she would make it through this, too.

The chemo and medications made her sick, and she couldn't get around well on her own. She gained a lot of weight. Eventually, I had to put her in a rehabilitation center because she couldn't get around on her own. She kept falling and wasn't able to walk. Her health spiraled downhill. Eventually, she refused to take the treatments. How could I make her do radiation and the chemo if it made her so sick? We all knew what that meant. I tried my best to make her room at the nursing home the best place I could. I hung beautiful pictures and brought her flowers. I stacked a shelf with tons of snacks that she wanted.

Mom was always the coolest one in the room. She was always well-liked and made friends easily. Even the caregivers and staff became her friends. I selected a nursing home close to my niece, Brandy, Angie's daughter. I wanted Mom to have family around her. Because I worked so much, it was hard to go every day to make sure she had everything she needed. I wasn't always able to make sure that she had the special food request she wanted that day or to bathe her, fix her hair, etc. In the new place, she had family all the time around her. Brandy was good to Mom.

She loved her so much and went every day until Mom had to go to the hospital.

Her cancer got progressively worse, and she was put on hospice care. The hospital employees were very accommodating. They knew we all wanted to be together when Mom passed. Mom was laughing, talking to us about whatever and everything up until the day she passed, surrounded by her family. Brandy's kids and grandkids, my kids and grandkids, and a friend's family, all sat around and had a good time with Mom.

We watched the slow decline as her breathing got slower. The end was coming closer, and we all knew it. We all sat around her bed crying. I wasn't crying yet because I had to be the strong one for everyone, just as I always was. On the inside, however, tears streamed down my heart because I was crying so hard. I held my mom in my arms as best I could while she lay in bed. I whispered in her ear "Mom, I forgive you for everything. It's OK to go. You're gonna be OK. Angie is waiting for you." I knew that would get her going. She would have her sidekick once again.

It seemed like it took forever for Mom's breathing to stop. Each break between her breaths, we all thought that was the last one. We didn't want her to die, of course, but we wanted the pain to stop. I whispered in her ear many times, "it's OK, Mom. It's OK. I told you I would always take care of you." And I did. I took care of her as best I could do, until her last breath.

I took care of my mom for over twenty years. I tried to do what I could for her. I didn't want her to go without anything. She got mad at me so many times, yet I know she was so proud of me. She was so proud of me for the choices I made in life and for the things I always gave to others. She knew I worked hard and tried my best to take care of my family. I grew up to be the caretaker of my whole family, and I was OK with that. So many people ask me why I took care of her when she didn't me. She was my mom, that's why. I love you, mom.

13

The Way Forward

As I reflect on my life now, I realize that for all of my bad choices, the best decision I made was to forgive—starting with myself. For years I held on to tremendous guilt for allowing my children to be abused. It wasn't until I started counseling that I understood that I was a victim. Because of all my bad choices, I felt I deserved all of the terrible things that happened to me. Now, I've learned to accept the fact that I'm not perfect. I'm the product of all the things which have happened to me, but I have a choice. And I choose to forgive those who hurt me. I think this is why I am always happy. I don't hold on to anger or resentment.

Even though I suffered a lot of abuse from my family I still love and forgive them. I wish I would have had a dad who would have helped me fix a flat tire, move furniture, or made me feel special—but that never happened. My dad, even when he was dying, never said that he was sorry. I don't want to be like that. I thank God for all of the good things that have happened to me (mainly my children), but also the bad things. It made me who I am.

I still hold onto a picture from when I was a young girl with Old Maw, my mom, Angie, and Amy. It's hard to believe that I'm the only one left! My mom died in August 2018, and Amy died six months later in 2019. Although it took me years, I learned to forgive them, too, for how they treated me. None of them had an easy life, either.

The willingness to forgive and move forward ALWAYS brings freedom.

Godsends

When my younger two children entered middle school, they had the opportunity to be part of a Big Brothers and Big Sisters program. God certainly knew what He was doing when he paired Shy and Dylan with the Hayden family. Dan and Jane Hayden were an amazing couple who grew up in very good homes and didn't have children of their own. The Haydens showed my kids how to do things in the right way—things that I never knew. They taught them how to do their homework, study for a test, and even how to keep a checkbook. They also instructed the kids on how to speak properly.

The Haydens took Shy and Dylan places on vacation that I never could. They gave them a life that I couldn't give them, and I am so happy that they were able to share so much with them. Yes, I was a little jealous at first. I felt inadequate that I couldn't show them the things they did. But, in the end, my heart is overwhelmed with gratefulness and joy because of them. Mr. and Mrs. Hayden still never forget a birthday or holiday. They make sure my children always get a card. I always said I wish I could be Jane. She's so smart and so organized. She's got it going on.

Jane's mother, Joyce, was beautiful as well. I met her years later when Jane asked me to help with her mom's in-home care. It's crazy because my kids Dylan and Shy knew her for years. Once I got to know her, I thanked her for raising such a good daughter to help mentor my children. I fell in love with Joyce; she was an awesome individual. She even inspired me to write this book. I feel privileged for the opportunity to care for her during her last year on earth. Joyce died in 2021.

Final Thoughts

As I look back on all of the crazy things that happened during my life, I realized that only I had the power to break the cycle of abuse. Many people have judged me for what happened to my girls, but I didn't "allow" my children to be abused. This happened while I was in prison. I realize now that my children NEVER should have been released to James.

But even before I got out of prison, I knew I had to find a way to escape this evil or he would have killed us all. When I tried to break free from his grip, he held my family at gunpoint. Until someone is in that very same position, they have no idea how they would respond.

I'm proud of who I am today. Determined to break the curse on my family, I often used tough love with my children. I'm reminded of an incident that happened when my son Dylan was 16. He ran with the wrong people and made some bad choices. One day, he took his sister Shy's truck and drove a few blocks while he was drinking. I called the courthouse and asked for him to be on probation. Since he was already in the system, they were able to accommodate me. I know that sounds terrible for a mother to turn in her own son, but I wanted to scare him straight.

Apparently, it worked! Dylan joined the Army over 7 years ago and is becoming the father to his daughter that he never had.

Years later I ran into the judge who sentenced Dylan, Judge Lucy Goffinet. She and her family would come into the diner where I waitressed for over 20 years. Even though I said some inappropriate things to her at the time (which I regret), I always treated them as I did all of my customers—with respect and great service. I always talked to her son. He smiled brightly every time he saw me.

One day around Christmas, this same judge came up to me at the diner. Even though I didn't wait on them that day she approached me, hugged me tight, and said "thank you." When she handed me the generous tip she had rolled up in her hand, I asked what was it for? She said that she wanted to thank me for treating *her* son so well. What an amazing feeling! I'm grateful for her kindness.

I'm very proud of all of my children: Ches, Brittany, Shy, and Dylan. My kids make me feel loved and valued. Each one has made amazing choices to break free from the chains which tried to entangle them. They, too, have reversed the curse in their own lives.

I feel very grateful for all the amazing people in my life. Tina Wright, my best friend for over 40 years, was always there to support me through the hard times. My boss, Joe Daum, who employed me off and on for over 20 years. Joe has always been an awesome mentor to me.

My vision is to help and encourage women who have suffered abuse. I want to help younger people set a course of positive thought. They need to understand that they are a victim and to forgive themselves first. Once they do this, they can begin to heal the pain and live an awesome life. They need to know that someone understands them and that they are going to be OK.

I want to give back, and this book is the first step. I hope that my story will inspire you. YOU have the ability to make better choices! YOU are not defined by what happened to you, or the bad decisions you've made in the past. Regardless of who you are, you can move forward from the pain of your past. You, too, can be UNDONE.

Contact Dottie

Dottie would love to hear from you! If you have questions or would like to have her speak to your group, please email her at the email below.

happydazies99@gmail.com

If you wish to purchase this book in bulk, reduced rates are available.

Made in USA - Kendallville, IN
89988_9798986215112
03.19.2024 2227